MANHATTAN PUBLIC LIBRARY DISTRICT

3 8001 00014 3234

W9-BUA-988

MANHATTAN PUBLIC LIBRARY
DISTRICT
PO BOX 53
240 WHITSON ST.
MANHATTAN, IL 60442
815-478-3987

Christmas in Today's Germany

Christmas in Today's Germany

Christmas Around the World
From World Book

World Book, Inc.
a Scott Fetzer company

Chicago London Sydney Toronto

MANHATTAN PUBLIC LIBRARY DIST

Staff
World Book Publishing

Publisher
William H. Nault

President
Daniel C. Wasp

Editorial

Vice President, General Publishing
Dominic J. Miccolis

Administrative Director
Roberta Dimmer

Managing Editor
Maureen Mostyn Liebenson

Associate Editor
Karen Zack Ingebretsen

Permissions Editor
Janet T. Peterson

Director of Research
Mary Norton

Researcher
Lynn Durbin

Art

Art Director
Wilma Stevens

Senior Editorial Artist
Deirdre Wroblewski

Director of Photography
John S. Marshall

Photographs Editor
Sandra Dyrlund

Product Production

Vice President, Production and Technology
Daniel N. Bach

Director of Manufacturing/Pre-press
Sandra Van den Broucke

Manufacturing Manager
Barbara Podczerwinski

Pre-press Production
Randi Park
Joann Seastrom
Julie Tscherney

Proofreaders
Anne Dillon
Karen Lenburg
Daniel J. Marotta

1996 Printing

© 1993 World Book, Inc. All rights reserved. This volume may not be reproduced in whole or in part in any form without prior written permission from the publisher.

World Book, Inc.
525 W. Monroe
Chicago, IL 60661

World Book Publishing and World Book Direct Marketing wish to thank the following individuals for their contributions to *Christmas in Today's Germany:* Jutta Birmele, Mechthilde Borries-Knopp, Rebecca Lauer, and Wolfgang Stein.

ISBN: 0-7166-0893-6
LC: 93-60510

Printed in Mexico

2 3 4 5 6 7 8 9 10 99 98 97 96

Contents

The land where many Christmas customs began

Throughout the world, families celebrate Christmas according to their regional culture and tradition. Certain traditions, however, have become widespread, and are enjoyed by people of various nations. For German families, Christmas traditions are particularly special, because many of them—including Christmas trees, Advent wreaths and calendars, and gingerbread houses—began in their homeland centuries ago. Many of our favorite Christmas carols and aspects of the Santa Claus tradition also come from Germany.

Today, Christmas is the biggest and most important holiday of the year in Germany. The Christmas season takes up more than a month, and includes a wide variety of celebrations. Throughout the country, Germans share many Christmas customs. Nearly everyone celebrates four main holidays—St. Nicholas Day, Christmas, New Year's Day, and Epiphany. But because Germany has many regional cultures, there are also many smaller holidays and customs observed in unique ways in different places.

Let's take a closer look at Christmas in Germany to see how it all began.

A brightly lit Christmas tree adorns the steps of a church in the city of Hamburg. A universal symbol of the season, the Christmas tree originated in Germany during the 1500's.

A young German boy helps his father carry home the family Christmas tree, which will be decorated on Christmas Eve.

The first Christmas tree

The Christmas tree, as we know it, developed from the custom of bringing evergreen boughs into the home during the dark, cold days of early winter. German people have practiced this custom for hundreds of years. Some people trace the practice to the ancient Romans, who celebrated a holiday called Saturnalia in December. They brought the branches of evergreen trees into their homes during that feast. The Germans may have made this Roman custom part of their Christmas celebrations after the two cultures came into contact in the 100's B.C.

But even before that time, Germanic tribes in northern Europe used evergreens in their rituals. These tribes celebrated a winter period called the Twelve Nights. In those ancient days, people believed in evil spirits. During the Twelve Nights, Germanic people tried to scare off

place candles near evergreen branches. Centuries later, a pine tree replaced the branches, and Christmas tree lights came to symbolize Jesus Christ, the Light of the World.

During the 1300's and 1400's, people in Germany celebrated a feast on December 24 in honor of Adam and Eve. During this feast, they held religious plays that centered around a "Paradise Tree"—a fir tree decorated with apples. These trees were set up in churches or outdoors. Although the plays gradually died out, the Paradise Trees remained popular, and some people may have started putting them up in their homes. Over time, the fir tree came to be a Christian symbol, adorned with small white wafers to represent the *Eucharist* (Holy Communion). Soon, people made cookies shaped like religious figures to hang on the tree. In this way, the apples of the Paradise Tree led to the wide variety of decorations that we hang on Christmas trees today.

Evergreens were not the only popular display in Germany, however. Some Germans built wooden pyramids which have sometimes been called "poor man's Christmas trees." The Christmas pyramid consisted of a series of wooden shelves arranged one above the other in the shape of a tree. Candles, small gifts, and fruit decorated each shelf. Sometimes people added elaborate carvings and figures, creating an impressive display that was anything but a "poor man's Christmas tree."

these spirits with grotesque masks and noisemakers. They also used evergreen branches to protect their homes. Because evergreen trees thrived in winter when other trees appeared to die, these tribal people thought evergreen branches had the magical power to ward off life-threatening spirits. According to custom, lights also had the power to guard against the demons, since light drives away darkness. As time passed, people began to

Many fascinating legends explain the origin of the Christmas tree. Here and on the following pages are just a few of these delightful myths.

The Saint Boniface legend

In the 700's, Saint Boniface, an English missionary in Germany, chopped down an oak tree that was used in pagan rituals involving human sacrifice. According to legend, a fir tree immediately sprang from the oak tree's stump. Thereafter Saint Boniface used the fir tree as a symbol of his faith.

The Martin Luther legend

According to an old tale, the Protestant reformer Martin Luther went walking through a forest one starry Christmas Eve. Crisp white snow covered the evergreen boughs along his path, and stars shone brightly above him. Luther was so enchanted by the beauty of the scene that he cut down a small fir tree and brought it home for his family. To represent the twinkling stars, he placed candles on its branches—and the Christmas tree was born. Although Luther left no record of this event, the story became so widespread that many Catholics of the time considered the Christmas tree a Protestant custom.

In Germany today, towering pyramid trees still grace some marketplaces and town squares during the Christmas season.

The Christmas tree we recognize today probably first appeared in Germany during the 1500's. According to one popular legend, Martin Luther, the great Protestant reformer, introduced Christmas trees into German homes in the early part of that century. By the 1600's, the candles, gifts, and fruit that adorned the pyramids were also hung on the Christmas tree. Over time, bright paper roses, apples, wafers, and candies be-

came the usual decorations. By the mid-1800's, the Christmas tree was common throughout Germany. Its popularity grew first among Protestants, probably because of the Martin Luther legend. Roman Catholics were still reluctant to follow what many felt was a Protestant custom. Of

A mother and child admire the Old World craftsmanship of hand-carved nutcrackers, incense burners, and pyramid trees produced at the Olbernhau arts and crafts workshop.

Saint Nicholas pays a visit to children, adults, and even the family dog in this 1890's etching.

course, today the tree has become a universal symbol of Christmas, and is no longer connected to any specific religion.

Christmas trees were rare outside of Germany until the early 1800's, when German immigrants brought the custom to the United States. Christmas trees began to spread through Europe in the 1840's, when Queen Victoria of Great Britain and her German husband, Prince Albert, put up a Christmas tree for their children. At about the same time, the German Princess Helen carried the custom to Paris when she married the Duke of Orleans.

Santa Claus and the story of Saint Nicholas

To American children, Santa Claus is such a popular fellow, so widely recognized by his thick beard and red suit, that it seems he must have brightened children's hearts everywhere since the beginning of time. But Santa, as we know him today, is less than 200 years old, and many countries have very different traditions of gift-giving in the Christmas season. Many of the traditions about Santa came from stories about a real person named Saint Nicholas. In many places in Europe, Saint Nicholas is still an important part of the

And a legend of long, long ago...

A tale from the 900's says that when Christ was born, all the forest animals began to speak and all the snow-laden trees bore fruit, in homage to the newborn King. But there was one fir tree who was too small to take part. The other trees apparently thought the fir tree was too homely to be seen, so they tried to hide it. But the Lord above thought otherwise, and he sent stars from heaven to decorate the branches of the little fir tree. Today, our glittering Christmas trees reflect the brilliance of that small fir tree.

Christmas characters, villains, and mythical creatures

Germany has produced an enormous number of Christmas characters over the centuries. Some are obviously intended to encourage good behavior among children. Others simply delight the imagination.

In pre-Christian times, the Germanic people believed in a number of Norse gods. Some of these gods had habits that are similar to those of modern Christmas characters. In those days, German children awaited the arrival of Odin, the king of the gods. He rode an eight-legged horse named Sleipnir through the forests, bringing gifts to the people. Thor, the god of thunder and lightning, rode through the sky in a chariot pulled by two white goats—Cracker and Gnasher. He was also a generous soul who lavished gifts on people. And Frau Berchta, the goddess of hearth and home, was another source of abundant gifts. Frau Berchta is also called by other names, including Bertha, Perchta, and Hertha. Nowadays most of these grand characters have disappeared and, unfortunately,

some less friendly characters have taken their place.

People in southern Germany have to watch out for a weird creature named Krampus. He has a long tail, a red snake-like tongue, and carries a sinister-looking basket on his back. If Krampus thinks someone has misbehaved, that person may wind up in Krampus' basket on Christmas Eve.

The Berchten runners may be the most scheming rascals of all. In a part of southern Germany called Bavaria, they travel the land, asking what people have done for them during the year. If people don't offer them gifts, these rogues make trouble. The Berchten runners often visit farms, wearing horrible masks and bragging about how much their "queen bee," Frau Berchta, has done for the crops.

Other frightening characters include Hans Muff, Butz, Hans Tripp, Klaubauf, Bartel, Budelfrau, Pelznickel, and Habersack. These creatures rarely bring presents, but they often leave lumps of coal or dirt—or even help themselves to the children's toys. They're unpredictable, disagreeable, and best avoided.

Young masked men posing as the Berchten runners roam the Bavarian countryside seeking gifts from the villagers.

A German mother reads a Christmas story to her children under a candlelit tree in the early 1900's.

Christmas season, and he is particularly popular among German children.

Saint Nicholas was a Christian bishop who lived in Asia Minor during the 300's. Saint Nicholas loved children, and was known for his great generosity. Over time, he became a legendary figure who rewards good children with gifts. He is often pictured with a bushy white beard, and wearing a long red robe and a tall pointed headdress. He usually carries a staff.

In Germany and other parts of Europe, it became a tradition for children to receive food or other gifts on St. Nicholas Day, December 6, or on the evening before. European immigrants, including the Dutch and the English, brought the tradition to America, where Nicholas gradually developed into the Santa we know today. The name Santa Claus comes from *Sinterklaas*, which is Dutch for Saint Nicholas.

German children receive gifts from other Christmas figures on Christmas Eve. According to one tradition, the gifts are sent by the *Christkind* (Christ child). This tradition is most

Members of the Regensburg Cathedral Sparrows, a youth choir, sing out a musical Christmas greeting outside a church in the Bavarian Alps.

important in southern Germany, where most of the people are Roman Catholic. In northern Germany, where most people are Protestant, parents say that the *Weihnachtsmann* (Christmas Man) brings presents on Christmas Eve. The Weihnachtsmann looks a lot like certain other gift-bringers—including Santa in the United States and Father Christmas in Great Britain.

German Christmas carols

Carols are an old and important part of German Christmas celebrations. We inherit many of our favorite Christmas carols from German culture.

Carols originate from early Latin hymns, which proclaimed the birth of Christ. But modern carols are generally more festive than hymns. Saint Francis of Assisi, who lived during the late 1100's and early 1200's, may have made an important contribution to the Christmas carol. Legend has it that Saint Francis, wondering how best to bring Christ's message to the people, wrote a song telling the story of Christ's birth in the stable. Others followed his lead in the centuries to

14

The traveling German singers may have inspired the custom of Christmas caroling that people enjoy today.

Martin Luther, who wrote many popular hymns, also wrote a beautiful Christmas song. He is said to have written "From Heaven Above to Earth I Come" while rocking his little daughter to sleep. This song still rings out from the dome of the Kreuzkirche in Dresden on Christmas morning. And of course the well-known "O Tannenbaum" ("O Christmas Tree") also originated in Germany.

Philipp Nicolai, pastor of a church in Unna (a town near Dusseldorf), wrote another great Christmas carol. A plague had recently killed many of his parishioners and he was deep in sorrow when a song suddenly came to him. This carol, "How Brightly Shines the Morning Star," was published in 1599.

Most of us are familiar with another famous Christmas carol, "Hark! The Herald Angels Sing." Charles Wesley of England composed an early version of the song in 1739. But it didn't become popular until more than 100 years later, when the words were set to a melody that German-born Felix Mendelssohn composed.

Christmas trees, decorations, and carols are just a few of the traditions that the German people have contributed through the ages. So there is little wonder that Christmas in Germany today is the biggest, brightest holiday of the year.

come, and the Nativity scene became the theme of many lovely carols. The Franciscans, the religious order Saint Francis founded, helped spread the tradition of singing carols about Christ's birth throughout Europe. Christmas carols became popular in Germany in about the 1300's.

During the Middle Ages in Germany, poor students traveled from house to house singing, in the hope of receiving small gifts. Wandering singers known as *Kurrende-Sänger* still go caroling in parts of Germany such as Saxony and Thuringia.

The land and people behind the traditions

Nestled in the heart of central Europe, Germany is the perfect setting for a white Christmas. Temperatures throughout most of the winter are near freezing, and a number of cities and towns are covered with a blanket of snow by Christmas Day.

During the Christmas season, Germany's towns and villages look like scenes from a Christmas card. Their snow-laden trees and picturesque houses shimmer with lights and garlands, and candles twinkle in the windows. Inside these houses, as early as November, someone may be making a gingerbread house, an Advent wreath, or an Advent calendar with all its doors ready for the children to open.

The German people make Christmas as happy and joyous as possible. They enjoy good food and serve it in abundance, especially at Christmas. Some of our most cherished Christmas goodies—including many Christmas cookies, the gingerbread house, and the gingerbread man—are German creations.

To become familiar with the German people and their contribution to Christmas, it helps to know something about their history and the origin of the holiday itself.

The glowing lights of a Christmas tree illuminate a mountaintop chapel, reflecting the peace and serenity of the season.

The introduction of Christmas

The real story of Christmas begins, of course, with the birth of Jesus Christ in Bethlehem. (The word *Christmas* comes from an early English phrase, *Cristes maesse*, meaning *Christ's Mass*.) Although no one knows for sure when Christ was born, most Christians celebrate His birthday on December 25.

The Gospels of Saint Luke and Saint Matthew in the New Testament tell about the birth of Christ. According to Luke, an angel appeared to shepherds outside the town of Bethlehem and told them the good news. Matthew tells how the Three Wise Men, known as the Magi, followed a bright star that led them to the baby Jesus.

The first mention of December 25 as the birth date of Jesus occurred in A.D. 336 in an early Roman calendar. Historians believe that this date may have been influenced in part by pagan festivals held at that time of year in northern Europe, including

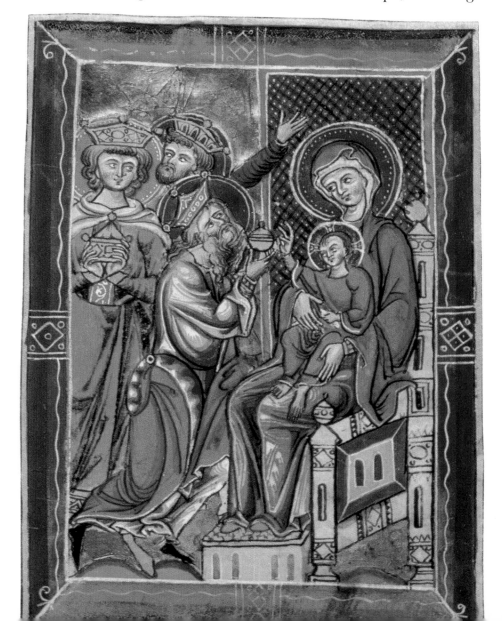

An illuminated manuscript page from a German lectionary depicts the adoration of the Magi. Lectionaries are books in which the New Testament is rearranged into readings for feast days.

High in the Bavarian Alps, the tradition of the Christmas play lives on as villagers reenact the Nativity.

what is now Germany. In addition, the ancient Romans celebrated their Saturnalia holiday in December. In the late 300's, however, Christianity became the official religion of the Roman Empire.

Christianity and the practice of celebrating Christmas spread to Germany in the 700's. The ancient Germanic tribes mixed many of their pagan rituals with the Christian ones and added a number of embellishments over the centuries. The Christmas celebration we know today is the happy result.

Ancient times in Germany

About 3,000 years ago, warlike tribes began to migrate from northern Europe into what is

now Germany. These primitive tribes lived by hunting, gathering, and farming. In the 100's B.C., they moved south to the Rhine and Danube rivers, the northern frontiers of the Roman Empire. The Romans called the people *Germani,* though that was the name of only one tribe. Eventually the main region where these tribes lived became known as *Germany.*

Germany inherited much of its mythology from these tribal people. They created such legendary figures as Thor, Odin, Frau Berchta, and even Knecht Ruprecht.

Many of these pagan beliefs and rituals became entwined with Christian traditions. For instance, while the candlelit

Young men wearing terrifying masks dance through German villages on St. Nicholas Day. In this ancient pagan custom, mothers give the costumed men gifts to keep them from frightening the children.

Advent wreath is a Christian symbol, the custom of bringing evergreen branches into the house during the winter months dates back to ancient times. These early people performed magic rites around the evergreen branches to ensure the return of vegetation in the spring. When the Germans became Christians in the 700's, they adapted certain old traditions to their new Christian beliefs.

The Germanic tribes also held many end-of-the-year festivals giving thanks to their gods for a rich harvest. The people prepared special foods, exchanged presents, and celebrated together with song and dance. As Christianity spread, these festivities continued as a part of Christmas tradition. By the 1100's, Christmas had become the most important religious festival in the land and Saint Nicholas had become the symbol of gift giving.

In 1517, a German monk called Martin Luther began to question some of the teachings and practices of the Roman Catholic Church. Many people—from nobles to peasants—joined his movement, which soon became known as the Reformation. Luther's followers were called *Protestants,* meaning those who protest. Protestantism soon spread from Germany to the rest of the world.

Many of the Reformation's effects on Germany were permanent. The nation became divided—the north becoming predominantly Protestant while the south and west remained Catholic. During the 1500's and 1600's, the Roman Catholic Church led its own reform, known as the Counter Reformation, and won back many of the people who had followed Luther. But Germany remained religiously divided.

After the Reformation, Protestants and Roman Catholics

In this Victorian engraving, a mother and daughter place candles on a tabletop Christmas tree—a German tradition which dates from the early 1700's.

in Germany continued to practice many of the same Christmas customs that their ancestors had for centuries. However, Protestants no longer followed many of the old customs associated with saints' days that the Catholic church celebrated during the Christmas season.

Recent history

Christmas became so much a part of German culture that not even the upheavals of the 20th century could dim its magic.

For several hundred years following the Reformation, Germany consisted of a collection of free cities and hundreds of separate states. Then, in the late 1600's, the powerful state of Prussia began to emerge. During the mid-1800's, the prime minister of Prussia, Otto von Bismarck, united most of Germany's states under Prussian leadership. This new German Empire was defeated in World War I (1914-1918), and a period of great political and economic unrest followed.

In 1933, Nazi leader Adolf Hitler came to power and soon began to establish a military dictatorship, rebuilding Germany's military force. In 1939, Hitler started World War II. Germany was again defeated. The four major Allied nations—France, Great Britain, the Soviet Union, and the United States—then divided Germany into zones of occupation. Even the capital city of Berlin was divided. In 1949, the British, French, and U.S. zones became the Federal Re-

Snow sledding remains as popular today with German children as it was during the 1940's, when this photograph was taken.

public of Germany, commonly called West Germany. That same year, the Soviet zone became the German Democratic Republic, known as East Germany.

West Germany was a parliamentary democracy with strong ties to Western Europe and the United States. East Germany was a Communist dictatorship dominated by the Soviet Union. While West Germans were free to celebrate Christmas as they always had, East German citizens were restricted by Communist philosophy, which discouraged all the religious aspects of Christmas. From 1945 until 1989, East Germans who wished to attend church services faced great difficulties, including the risk of discrimination. Attending church could ruin a person's career or prevent their admittance to a

university. There were no public displays of religious scenes, no Advent wreaths, and no religious Christmas songs. Many parents were even afraid to discuss religion with their children. Thus, a generation of East Germans grew up knowing little about the story of the birth of Christ, or the true significance of Christmas.

Nevertheless, the spirit of Christmas endured. It was still a time to share joy and love with family and friends. And although Christ was not publicly acknowledged, He certainly lived on in the hearts of the people. The East Germans gave presents to their loved ones and put up Christmas trees in their homes. East German artists continued to make the famous wooden pyramid trees with elaborate carvings and figures and exported them throughout the world. The Advent calendar became a "Christmas" calendar, Christmas fairs were still held, and people continued to enjoy a traditional Christmas feast.

However, many families were split up during this period. Because so many East Germans tried to flee to the West, the Communist regime built the Berlin Wall in 1961. This effectively isolated East Germany and cut off a major escape route. Very few East Germans were permitted to visit West German relatives—and then often only one at a time. The rest of the family had to remain behind to guarantee the traveler's return to East Germany. West Germans needed special permits to visit East Germany, and they had to pay a daily fee for staying there.

Every year on Christmas Eve, many West Berliners living near the Berlin Wall lit candles in their windows for East Berliners to see. The candles were a tribute to their fellow Germans and a way of saying *"Fröhliche Weihnachten"* (Merry Christmas) to those behind the wall.

In the late 1980's, reforms swept through the Soviet Union and other Communist nations, including East Germany. In 1989, the East German government finally allowed its citizens to travel freely—for the first time in 40 years.

With the end of travel restrictions, there was no longer any need for the Berlin Wall, and down it came. Soon, East Germans were allowed to form non-Communist political parties, and in March 1990, free elections gave non-Communists control of the government. Finally, on October 3, East and West reunited, becoming a single, free country once again.

Standing near the former Berlin Wall, Saint Nicholas and a young German man celebrate the end of travel restrictions in East Germany.

Today, all the German people are free to celebrate the true meaning of Christmas. They can take part in church services and other religious traditions. And they can spend as much time as they wish with their families, wherever they live.

The beauty and joy of the season can be seen everywhere, from the bustling, modern cities of Frankfurt and Berlin to quaint and peaceful villages in the countryside. Year after year, age-old customs that recall a distant, fascinating past are brought vividly to life and blended with newer traditions.

Christmas is a time of magic and merriment, and of wishes and dreams that come true. In days gone by, when Germany consisted of small, separate states, German children left their shoes by the chimney in hopes that Saint Nicholas would fill them with fruit, nuts, and candy. Today, Germany is one of the leading industrial nations in the world, and as the standard of living has risen, so have the expectations of its youngsters. Clothes, toys, books, sporting equipment, and computer games now appear on the "wish lists" of modern German children.

Mothers and fathers who want to fulfill their children's dreams often use their special Christmas bonus to buy presents to place under the tree. In recent years, German employers and trade unions have developed a bonus program so that employees may enjoy the pleasure of Christmas shopping without exceeding their budget. The

In her busy workshop, a German artist creates tiny replicas of pyramid trees—an early version of the Christmas tree popular during the mid-1600's.

Germany

North Sea

Baltic Sea

☆ *National Capital*
★ *State Capital*
• *City*

DENMARK

Kiel ★
Schleswig-
Holstein

• Rostock

Mecklenburg-
Western
Pomerania

Hamburg ★
Schwerin ★

• Emden
• Bremerhaven
Bremen
• Bremen ★

Hamburg

POLAND

Brandenburg

Lower Saxony

★ Hanover

Magdeburg ★

★ Berlin
Potsdam ★

Berlin

NETHERLANDS

North Rhine-
Westphalia

Saxony-Anhalt

Halle •

• Leipzig

Saxony

★ Düsseldorf

Dresden ★
Chemnitz
•

Cologne •

Erfurt ★
Thuringia

Bonn •

Hesse

• Suhl

CZECH
REPUBLIC

BELGIUM

Frankfurt
★ Wiesbaden

Rhineland-
Palatinate
Mainz ★

• Nuremberg

LUXEMBOURG

Saar
★ Saarbrücken

• Regensburg

Bavaria

FRANCE

★ Stuttgart

• Augsburg

Baden-
Württemberg

★ Munich

• Freiburg

AUSTRIA

SWITZERLAND

Today's Germany has an area of 137,358 square miles (355,754 square kilometers) and a population of more than 77 million people. Berlin is its capital and largest city.

bonus is considered part of an employee's wages, and is generally based on length of employment. Everyone, children and adults alike, looks forward to the time-honored tradition of gift giving. Yet the true spirit of Christmas—family togetherness, peace, love, and good will toward all—is never lost in this scenic country which gave the world its first Christmas tree.

A great German season

Most of the world's children have to wait until late December to celebrate Christmas—but not German children. Their Christmas season lasts for more than a month, from the start of Advent in late November to Epiphany, or Three Kings Day, on January 6. But even before Advent begins, German families celebrate another important holiday, St. Martin's Day, on November 11. Although it is a Roman Catholic feast day, Protestants in Germany observe it in honor of Martin Luther, who was born on November 10, the eve of St. Martin's Day. He was baptized the following day and named after the saint. St. Martin's Day—a holiday that rivals St. Nicholas Day and Christmas itself in the hearts of German children—is a colorful celebration, based on history, legend, and ancient tradition.

The brilliant lights of the Christkindlmarkt brighten the night sky above Nuremberg, where one of the first Christmas fairs took place more than 350 years ago.

The legend of Saint Martin is reenacted in the town square of Düsseldorf as part of the St. Martin's Day festivities.

Germany's Many Christmas Holidays

Germany celebrates four major holidays during the Christmas season—St. Nicholas Day, Christmas, New Year's, and Epiphany. But over the centuries, Germans have also celebrated a remarkable number of smaller holidays and regional customs. A listing of some of these observances appears here and on the following pages.

November 30—St. Andrew's Night

On this night, legend says that if a woman throws a shoe over her shoulder toward a door at midnight, and the shoe lands with its toe pointed toward the door, the woman will receive a marriage proposal the following year. Although Saint Andrew is the patron saint of Scotland, many German people also celebrate his special day.

Saint Martin was appointed bishop of Tours in A.D. 372, and over the centuries he became an important saint in Germany. During the Middle Ages, St. Martin's Day marked the start of the dark and cheerless transition from autumn to winter.

A legend tells how Saint Martin, then a Roman soldier, rode through the countryside one cold day and met a beggar who asked him for alms. As a soldier, Saint Martin had nothing of value to give the poor man. All he had was his cloak. So without hesitation, Saint Martin took off his cloak, cut it in two pieces, and gave one piece to the beggar. That night Saint Martin had a dream in which Christ appeared and said, "Martinus, who is not yet baptized, protect me against the cold." Saint Martin then devoted his life to God.

On St. Martin's Day, children receive small gifts, eat goodies, and show off their artistic talents. Children in parts of western and central Germany walk in colorful processions after dark. Many of them carry homemade lanterns, and some even carry hollowed-out turnips, as their ancestors did long ago. Many of these lanterns are highly artis-

28

Just as their ancestors before them did, German children celebrate St. Martin's Day by carrying homemade lanterns in colorful, after-dark processions.

tic—the result of weeks of work. Most are made of cardboard cut into the shapes of balloons, stars, and other objects in beautiful, intricate designs. Transparent colored paper covers this basic shape, and a candle glows inside. Some lanterns show scenes from Saint Martin's life, while others depict plants and animals. Children usually carry these lanterns on long poles, lighting up the night. Musicians sometimes follow the children, and everyone joins in singing "St. Martin's songs." In some towns, at the end of the procession, the children gather to watch a reenactment of the old legend. To their great delight, "Saint Martin" often rides in on a real horse. Reenacting the story of Saint Martin— especially the division of his cloak—teaches children to be kind to less fortunate people.

Today, children often receive a currant bun on St. Martin's Day. These buns, made of high-quality leavened dough, are usually shaped like a person, animal, plant, or other object.

Long before the legend of Saint Martin appeared, the ancient Germanic tribes celebrated this time of year with great bonfires. They believed the bon-

The world's largest Advent wreath takes up a city block in Münster. Advent wreaths are a cherished tradition throughout Germany.

First Sunday of Advent
Advent begins on the Sunday nearest November 30 and continues until Christmas Eve. People light one of the four candles on the Advent wreath each Sunday of Advent.

December 4—St. Barbara's Day
On St. Barbara's Day, according to an old custom, some Germans still put cherry, elder, or peat branches in water and set them in a warm place. If the branches bloom for Christmas, this will deter misfortune in that home in the coming year.

fires would keep their fields fertile. This ritual eventually became part of the St. Martin's Day festivities, which are still celebrated with light and fire in some areas of Germany.

For weeks before St. Martin's Day, children collect old baskets, branches, cardboard boxes, straw—and almost anything else that will burn. They pile them up and create a giant bonfire on St. Martin's Eve. Often these bonfires can be seen for miles. The "Martinmas" fire was a more popular custom than the lantern procession until the 1900's, when people began to worry that the fires might spread.

After the procession and the performance, the children go singing through the town. Their songs ask for small gifts from neighbors and shopkeepers. Usually their efforts are rewarded with apples, nuts, candies, biscuits, and sometimes even money. And the louder they sing, the more they get.

St. Martin's Day is celebrated with many local variations. In some Protestant areas, songs are sung in honor of Martin Luther. In the Bohemian and Bavarian forests, St. Martin's Day is dedicated to shepherds. And in many areas, it is customary to serve a "Martinmas Goose" for dinner.

Only 45 days until Christmas

As the embers of St. Martin's Day fires fade, the German people look forward to Advent, the official start of the Christmas season. In the Christian calendar, Advent is the month before Christmas, beginning with the Sunday nearest November 30. The name comes from the Latin term *Adventus Redemptoris*, meaning *The Coming of the Savior*. People in towns and cities all over Germany celebrate Advent, or *Lichtwochen* (light weeks), with great joy.

Holiday preparations begin in earnest on the first Sunday of Advent. People string lights and garlands on lampposts and across every storefront. Families begin baking festive cookies and start doing their Christmas shopping. All sorts of specialty shops and markets tempt young and old alike with dazzling displays. And the Advent wreath makes its annual debut.

The Advent wreath is one of Germany's most widespread customs. It consists of four candles placed within a wreath of braided fir twigs. People light the candles in succession, one on each Sunday of Advent, so that all four burn in Jesus' honor by Christmas Day.

The Advent calendar is also a popular tradition throughout Germany. Each Advent calendar has 24 tiny doors representing the 24 days of December leading up to Christmas. Every day the children open one of the doors to find a tiny Christmas scene. The last door, opened on Christmas Eve, usually reveals the baby Jesus in the manger.

The Advent calendar dates back to the 1800's. Today, many German families make their own Advent calendars. These handmade versions are often beautifully crafted, and a source of great pride.

The Advent calendar was originally intended to teach children about Christ's birth and the meaning of Christmas. Of course, parents soon discovered that it could also be used to inspire patience—and good behavior—among children who can hardly wait for Christmas to arrive.

December 5–St. Nicholas Eve
On the evening of December 5, Saint Nicholas delivers candy, nuts, and fruit to the children. Saint Nicholas often travels with a frightening companion—Knecht Ruprecht— who brings switches instead of gifts. Saint Nicholas, a bishop in Asia Minor during the A.D. 300's, is the patron saint of children and sailors.

Illustrated Advent calendars are a special delight for children, as a new surprise awaits behind each of the 24 doors.

The legendary Saint Nicholas is a welcome sight—but beware of his attendant, Knecht Ruprecht, who punishes naughty children with a switch!

December 6–St. Nicholas Day
On this day the children wake to find their shoes filled with candy, nuts, and fruit—gifts from Saint Nicholas.

December 21–St. Thomas' Day
On this day, some Germans honor Saint Thomas the Apostle. They may bake a special fruitcake or iced currant buns on St. Thomas Day.

December 21 or 22–The Winter Solstice
This day, the shortest of the year in the Northern Hemisphere, marks the official beginning of winter.

December 24–Christmas Eve
Christmas Eve is a holy day, and many Germans attend church in the early afternoon or the evening. People light beautiful Christmas trees and children look forward to opening gifts.

This custom became so popular that East German parents adapted it to comply with Communist restrictions. The Advent calendar became the "Christmas" calendar—its religious scenes replaced by winter scenes, animals, and Christmas decorations. Now that the nation is reunited, German children can enjoy any Advent calendar they choose.

Saint Nicholas comes early

Only a few doors on the Advent calendar are open when it's time for Saint Nicholas to arrive. Saint Nicholas is honored on December 6, but in many parts of Germany the festivities begin the night before—St. Nicholas Eve.

On that night, Saint Nicholas visits the homes of children. Some say he rides around the countryside on a white pony, carrying two bags. One bag is full of rewards and the other contains switches. That night children go to bed anxiously awaiting his judgment, because Saint Nicholas knows whether they have been good or bad. On St. Nicholas Day, good children awake to find toys, apples, candies, and nuts. But those who

32

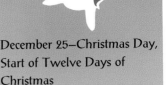

have misbehaved will find only switches. In many parts of Germany, children put out shoes for Saint Nick to fill with rewards. In other regions, Saint Nicholas may visit them in person, on December 5 or 6.

The legendary Knecht Ruprecht often comes with Saint Nick. But Ruprecht is rarely welcome. Some say he has a filthy beard that reaches the floor and wears a long dark coat made of animal hides. Ruprecht punishes naughty children by swatting them with his switch. He might also tell Saint Nicholas that certain children don't deserve presents. Those children will have to wait another year.

Today in a few parts of southern Germany, people still light bonfires in honor of Saint Nicholas on December 5. The bonfires probably began as a pagan ritual and were later adapted to fit Christian customs. These Saint Nicholas fires are always lit after dark, and young and old alike sing and dance around them.

The community usually selects someone to play the part of Saint Nicholas and lead the procession to the bonfire. This "Saint Nicholas" is easy to recognize by his bushy white beard, his long robe, his tall, pointed headdress, and his staff.

The "Riddle-Raddle Men"

In an area called Berchtesgaden, which lies in the Bavarian Alps of southern Germany, the people carry out a centuries-old tradition on St. Nicholas Day.

In pre-Christian times, people believed that demons and evil spirits inhabited the mountain valleys in winter. According to legend, these evil spirits would stay for the entire year unless they were driven out. Germanic tribes of the region had a ritual to scare away the demons, and it is followed to this day. Single men in the valley rise early in the morning and transform themselves from ordinary mortals into *Buttenmandelhaut* (Riddle-Raddle men). *Butten* is an old German word meaning rattle and shake, and that's exactly what the Riddle-Raddle men do.

December 25—Christmas Day, Start of Twelve Days of Christmas

Throughout Germany, people celebrate the holiest day of the year—Christ's birthday—with special church services, family reunions, and much festivity. The Twelve Days of Christmas or Holy Twelve Nights are said to foreshadow the year ahead. For example, events of the first day predict what January will be like, and those of the second foretell how February will fare.

In the Bavarian Alps, Riddle-Raddle men appear on St. Nicholas Day to scare away demons lurking in the mountain valleys.

December 26—Second Day of Christmas, St. Stephen's Day

The German people have the happy tradition of celebrating Christmas over two days. The second day of Christmas is also St. Stephen's Day. Saint Stephen is the patron saint of horsemen, and many towns and villages in southern Germany hold mounted processions.

To begin, the single men retreat to a barn, where they cover themselves in large sheafs of straw, secured around their waists with a rope. Then they put on masks with long red tongues, and arm themselves with cowbells, rattles, and other noisemakers. When the time is right, Riddle-Raddle men burst from the barn and dance madly down the valley, waving their noisemakers above their heads. They look like giant straw men—a strange and colorful sight—and the din they make can be heard all over the countryside.

Before they go from house to house, however, the Riddle-Raddle men take part in a Christian ceremony dedicated to Saint Nicholas, who also makes an appearance to offer a blessing. Afterward, a farmer's wife, who provided the straw, sprinkles the crowd with holy water. And then Saint Nicholas and the Riddle-Raddle men go from house to house with gifts for the children. Sometimes Saint Nicholas reads each child's good and bad deeds from a book and delivers an eloquent speech on the merits of being good.

Next comes the part of the ritual that the Riddle-Raddle men have been eagerly awaiting. It's time for them to playfully pick up all the single women in the household and carry them outside. Just about everyone is entertained by this boisterous

A dazzling array of handcrafted ornaments fills one of the more than 100 booths at the Christkindlmarkt in Nuremberg.

event. And it has become one of Germany's most vivid rural celebrations.

Christkindlmarkt (Christ Child's Fair)

Around the time that the first Advent candle is lit, Christmas fairs open throughout Germany. At these fairs, shoppers may choose from a dazzling array of Christmas merchandise: ornaments and toys; religious figurines and Nativity scenes; and candies, gifts, and Christmas trees. Often musicians play, and people put on puppet shows and plays.

The most famous of these fairs is the *Christkindlmarkt* in Nuremberg, where one of the first Christmas fairs took place more than 350 years ago. It gained such popularity that some 1,500 horse-drawn carts once arrived for the Nuremberg Christkindlmarkt in one day. Today, about 1 million shoppers come from all over the world.

Walking through the Nuremberg market is a delightful experience for everyone, but children seem to enjoy it most of all. More than 100 booths fill the marketplace, each bright with Christmas lights. Vendors offer roasted almonds and chestnuts, gingerbread houses, smoked sausage, wonderful toys and trinkets, and all types of wooden nutcrackers. Holiday music fills the air, and the scent of fir trees is all around. This great fair truly offers something for every visitor.

Today almost every German town hosts a Christmas fair, and many are quite spectacular, es-

Gingerbread houses, a much-loved German tradition, are great fun to make—and even greater fun to eat!

pecially those in Munich, Hamburg, Bremen, and Frankfurt. But the Nuremberg fair remains the largest and most impressive.

Preparations for the big day

The German people begin their Christmas preparations weeks in advance. Of these preparations, cooking ranks among the most important. Germans are renowned for their traditional dishes, and at Christmastime, they spare no pains.

During the Christmas season, you can find elaborate gingerbread houses and gingerbread

December 28—Feast of the Innocents

Holy Innocents' Day marks the time when King Herod murdered innocent children in Jesus Christ's homeland. Long ago, German children carried switches and pretended to swat adults on this day. According to the tradition, the adults gave the children small cakes to pacify them.

The end of the old year
and the start of the new! Ex-
citement grows all over Germany as midnight approaches.
Then bells ring, firecrackers
flare, champagne flows, and
people usher in the new year
with lots of music and danc-
ing. A hot, spiced drink called
Sylvesterabend punch is
often served. December 31
also honors Pope Sylvester I.

men in every bakery, but many
people like to make their own.
And the children love to help—
this is one chore they enjoy. German children have great fun cov-
ering gingerbread houses with
white icing like snow, making
doors out of candy canes, and
sprinkling everything with colored sugar. And when it's finished, a gingerbread house is even
more fun to eat. Creative children may bake gingerbread San-
tas and a host of animals. Candied lemon, orange peel, and
raisins make wonderful faces.

Some gingerbread houses
are called "witch houses." The

Grimm brothers immortalized
the witch house in their classic
fairy tale "Hansel and Gretel."

Germans bake a wide variety
of Christmas cookies, biscuits,
and cakes. The recipes for these
sweets have been passed down
for generations. Perhaps the
most popular Christmas treats
are honeyed cakes and biscuits,
such as *Lebkuchen* (gingerbread),
Pfeffernüsse (ginger cookies), and
Aachener Printen (Aachen almond
biscuits).

But the most famous German
specialty is marzipan. The main
ingredients of this delicious treat
are roasted almonds and sugar.
The almonds are ground and
mixed with sugar and other ingredients, shaped into various
forms, glazed, and baked. People often decorate their Christmas trees with marzipan. It is a
delicate confection that pleases
the eye as much as the palate.
For hundreds of years, only the
rich could afford marzipan, because its ingredients were scarce
and hence very expensive. Today,
Germany gets large shipments
of almonds from California, and
nearly every household serves
marzipan at Christmas. Certain
parts of Germany, especially
Lübeck, are famous for their
delicious marzipan.

A few weeks before Christmas, many German people put
up the family *crèche*, or Nativity
scene. The crèche is one of Germany's most cherished Christmas customs.

Many people believe Saint
Francis of Assisi created the first
crèche to increase his congrega-

Workers in a marzipan factory form the sweet confection, which is made of almond paste, into miniature fruits, vegetables, animals, and other shapes. Marzipan is Germany's most famous Christmas candy.

Crèches, which were brought to Europe by Franciscan and Dominican monks, began to appear in German homes around 1700.

tion's understanding of the Bible. He believed that a model of the scene in the stable where Christ was born would bring the story to life for his people. The idea caught on, and many churches began to erect Nativity scenes at Christmas. Today churches still construct crèches featuring life-sized figures of the infant Jesus with Mary, Joseph, and the Three Wise Men, as well as sheep, oxen, and shepherds.

In the Middle Ages, most German people knew little about Christ's birthplace, and their homemade crèches often reflected this lack of knowledge. Instead, they used their imagination or their own culture as a model for their crèches. These crèches often had huge barbar-ian figures—dressed in furs and carrying lances—standing over the baby Jesus. In some crèches from the 1700's, the shepherds wore wooden shoes, which were common in Germany at that time, and Mary even wore a bonnet. These early influences can still be seen in some modern-day crèches.

Once Nativity scenes appear in German homes and church-es, the Christmas season is definitely underway. As December 25 draws nearer, there is much to be done—presents to buy, parties to attend, and even more food to prepare. The spirit of Christmas has spread, warming shops and streets, homes and schools, and churches throughout the land.

January 6–Epiphany
Epiphany marks the end of the Christmas season. Many parties, special festivals, and processions take place on this holiday, which is also known as Twelfth Night or the Festival of the Three Kings. In certain towns, groups of boys who represent the Three Wise Men parade through the streets, singing "Star Songs." They usually receive food, drink, and donations for the needy from their audiences.

Advent wreaths are made of bound fir twigs and often decorated with pine cones, ribbons, and artificial snow.

Christian Roots of Germany's Most Beloved Traditions

Germany's many Christmas traditions are a wonderful mixture of age-old pagan rituals and Christian beliefs. Passed along from generation to generation, these traditions add a special meaning to the season's celebrations. Those traditions whose roots can be traced to the arrival of Christianity in Germany also reflect the deep, abiding faith of the German people.

In homes and churches throughout the country, the Advent wreath has come to symbolize the joyous anticipation leading to Christmas. Although the origin of the Advent wreath remains a mystery, the custom of observing Advent dates from the A.D. 500's. At that time, the six weeks before Christmas were a time of fasting and penitence as a way of honoring the coming Nativity. Under the influence of the Roman Catholic Church, the season was gradually reduced to four weeks. Today, in homes throughout Germany, the lighting of the Advent wreath brings with it a time of contemplation amid the hustle-bustle of shopping, baking, and decorating.

One of the four candles on the Advent wreath is lit on each of the four Advent Sundays as it begins to get dark in the afternoon. During the lighting ceremony, a family member reads a Christmas poem or story.

Children eagerly anticipate the arrival of Saint Nicholas, who brings presents for them in his sack.

In most German homes, the Advent wreath remains on the dining room table throughout the holiday season. In churches and shops, Advent wreaths are often hung from the ceiling and festooned with ribbons. In many German cities and towns, churches and private groups also hold special celebrations on the first Advent Sunday.

Less solemn, perhaps, but also firmly rooted in Christian tradition is the arrival of Saint Nicholas on his celebration day, December 6. One of the most popular saints in the Christian church, Saint Nicholas served as bishop of Myra in Lycia, which is now Turkey. Saint Nicholas is the patron saint of sailors, travelers, bakers, merchants, and children. On St. Nicholas Day, adults in towns and villages throughout Germany dress up in bishops' robes and go from house to house where children live. When a bell sounds, the children know that Saint Nicholas has arrived—but not alone.

A black figure in tattered clothes, most widely known as Knecht Ruprecht but also called Krampus, Pelzebock, Hans Muff, and Bartel, accompanies Saint Nicholas on his rounds. Together, Saint Nicholas and Knecht Ru-

Star singers go from house to house, performing for villagers and seeking donations for the needy.

precht question each child diligently: "Have you minded your parents? Have you said your prayers?" Children who have been good receive treats. But woe to the naughty ones, for they'll surely feel the sting of Knecht Ruprecht's switch!

One of the oldest Christian traditions takes place during Epiphany, a festival that commemorates the adoration of the infant Jesus by the Three Wise Men, who had come from the East. During the Middle Ages, popular plays about the wise men were performed throughout Europe. Although none of

these plays survived, one part of the performance has lived on—star singing.

On the Sunday closest to Epiphany, three young singers dress up as the wise men. Wearing crowns made of cardboard, the wise men and their retinue of singers go from door to door singing Epiphany carols. Gaspar, the Moorish king, carries a gold star on a pole. In small cases decorated with "jewels," the Three Wise Men collect money to be donated to missionary activities in the Third World—a most fitting way to bring Christ's message of peace and hope to others.

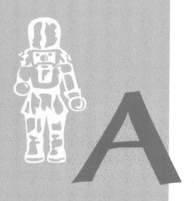

Christmas in Germany today

According to ancient folklore, there is more magic on Christmas Eve than ordinary people can imagine. River and well water turns into wine, animals speak and frozen trees blossom, mountains open to reveal precious stones, and the sound of church bells rings on the ocean floor. But only the pure of heart can witness these wonders. So most of us take simple pleasure in traditional Christmas celebrations.

For Germans everywhere, December 24 marks the height of the festivities. Shops and offices close around noon so that people can prepare for the evening gala ahead. And most traditional Christmas activities take place that night.

Christmas Eve is a magical day for children. Almost every German home has a tree, and many people put theirs up on that day. Families make it an exciting event for the children, surrounded in mystery and suspense.

A mother and her son decorate the family Christmas tree with shiny ornaments, candles, gingerbread figures, and icicles.

The magic and delight of the Christmas season are reflected in the happy faces of these two young children.

Parents usually decorate the Christmas tree behind closed doors, while the children wait expectantly in another room. Finally, after what seems to them an eternity, the children are allowed to enter. For a moment, the parents keep the room completely dark. And then they reveal the glittering Christmas tree in all its glory, brilliant with candles and shiny ornaments.

Many Germans also decorate their trees with gingerbread figures, a marzipan Saint Nicholas, gilded fruit and nuts, religious figures, gold stars, and angels. Pine scents the air as the family gathers around the tree to open their gifts and sing carols. In some areas, children hold *Wunderkerzen* (sparklers) as they stand around the tree. Outside, col-

ored lights often decorate the eaves of the house.

Children in Germany are not expected to wait until morning to open their gifts—they can do it on Christmas Eve. First, however, many parents read aloud the story of Christ's birth, so that the true spirit of Christmas is remembered. Afterward, the children are free to tear into their gifts. There may be electric trains, model toys, clothes, games, dolls, books, jewelry, and any number of other items. After everyone has opened their packages, the whole family joins in playing games.

By the time German families exchange their gifts, delicious aromas have been wafting through the house for hours, and the Christmas feast is ready at last. Many German families sit down to a dinner that resembles an elegant all-you-can-eat buffet. The table sparkles with the best silver and china, the candles are lit, and everyone is dressed for the occasion. The main course may be roast goose with apple-prune stuffing, though in days past they often served a roast pig. Some families prefer turkey or duck, while others serve carp, a traditional Christmas Eve dish since the Middle Ages. Monks used to keep special carp ponds to provide people with the fish for Christmas dinner, and some families still follow this age-old custom.

Germans also enjoy a wide variety of tempting side dishes. There may be *Spätzle* (noodle dumplings), *Königinpasteten* (meat-filled pastries), and green beans in *Zwiebelbutter* (onion butter). Other favorites include *Bayerisches Kraut* (Bavarian red cabbage) and *Kartoffelsalat* (potato salad). For dessert, there are Nuremburg spiced cakes, Silesian poppy seed stollen, Rhenish almonds, and Dresdner Christstollen—not to mention marzipan figures and cookies of every imaginable variety.

An old Protestant myth says that whoever does not eat well on Christmas Eve will be haunted by demons during the

A German family celebrates Christmas with a special feast in their dining room, topped off with a delectable variety of Christmas cakes and cookies for dessert.

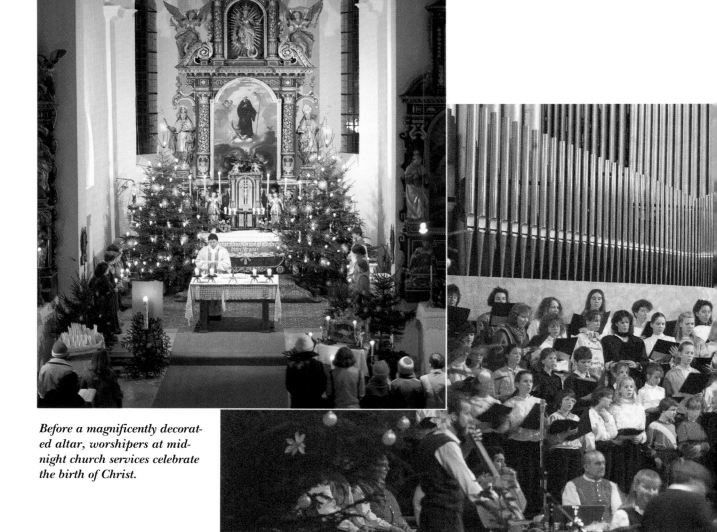

Before a magnificently decorated altar, worshipers at midnight church services celebrate the birth of Christ.

A church choir in Nuremberg sings favorite Christmas carols for the congregation.

night. Children and servants were always allowed to eat as much as they wanted, so Christmas Eve became known as *Dickbauch* (Fat Stomach). But even today, German doctors are bombarded with calls from patients suffering from "mysterious" stomach pain.

Every Christmas dinner includes fine German wines and liqueurs to toast everyone's health and prosperity in the coming year. Afterward, coffee or tea is served with yet more cakes and cookies—for those who still have the appetite.

Most German families start planning and preparing this feast weeks in advance. The Christmas dinner may take all day to cook, but many of the most popular dishes are easy to make.

Just before midnight, residents of the town of Berchtesgaden observe an unusual custom that is more than 300 years old. The Christmas Shooting Club fires off a round of shots in the sky, and the noise from the guns makes Christmas Eve seem like an American Independence Day. The gunshots are meant to scare off evil spirits and attract the good ones, including the Christ child. When all is silent once more, the church bells ring. Midnight Mass is about to begin.

also in southern Germany, small Christmas trees with burning candles are set on graves. In large cities, special buses take people to the cemeteries on Christmas Eve to visit the graves of loved ones.

In some parts of Germany, Christmas Eve is a time for fortunetelling. In Thuringia, for example, people pull a single straw from a thatched roof. If grains of corn cling to the straw, it means a good harvest lies ahead. People also beat fruit trees at midnight to ensure a better crop.

Throughout Germany, Christmas Eve is the holiest night of the year, and one of the most festive. Christmas Day is less eventful in German homes, but no less enjoyable. It is a time for relaxing and unwinding. Relatives often visit and share the spirit of the season. Children play and show off their gifts. Some families have a Christmas dinner. But the season hasn't ended, because December 25 is just "the first day of Christmas."

Christmas in East Germany— Past and Present

Christmas in former East Germany is radically different today. The fall of the Communist regime and the reunification of Germany have united families throughout the country.

In 1990, for the first time in more than 40 years, East German families were free to spend Christmas with their West German relations. Since then, families have enjoyed many holiday reunions, as sisters and brothers

Churches in Germany are usually packed on Christmas Eve. Many Germans attend services at midnight, while others go to church in the afternoon or evening. For many people, these services are the highlight of the Christmas celebration. The churches are aglow with candlelight and graced with a life-sized Nativity scene. During the Mass, the choir sings favorite Christmas songs, accompanied by organ music and violins.

In Berchtesgaden (a small town in southern Germany), church members place a lighted candle on every grave in the cemetery. In Oberammergau, met again and parents were once more united with their children.

Today, in reunified Germany, all German people are free to follow the religion of their choice. This religious freedom is a dramatic change for former East Germans. Now that people can attend services, many churches are crowded once again.

During the Communist regime, Christmas was merely a national holiday with no religious significance. Throughout East Germany, a generation of young people had little opportunity to learn the story of Christ's birth or be introduced to the teachings of Christ. Only people in small rural villages were bold enough to attend church or celebrate the true meaning of Christmas openly. Nevertheless, a few of the faithful always attended church on Christmas Eve. Although restrictions were relaxed on this one night, the East German government still frowned on church attendance.

Even under Communism, some East Germans displayed Advent decorations, particularly a type called a *Schwippbogen*. This decoration is a half circle of wood in which Christmas figures are carved and candles are lit.

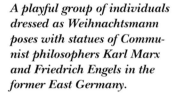

A playful group of individuals dressed as Weihnachtsmann poses with statues of Communist philosophers Karl Marx and Friedrich Engels in the former East Germany.

A glittering store display of animated figures delights the imaginations of young and old alike.

Many East Germans displayed them at home, and some villages put up large versions in the village square.

Except for the religious restrictions, Christmas in East Germany under the Communist regime was similar to Christmas in West Germany. Most families had a Christmas tree, crowds attended Christmas fairs, and people baked batches of Christmas cookies. There was plenty of feasting and shopping as well.

Children in East Germany looked forward to St. Nicholas Day as much as West German children did. On the evening of December 5, they too put out their shoes for Saint Nicholas to fill with candies during the night. They spent several hours cleaning their shoes, for their parents said Saint Nicholas wouldn't leave a gift if they didn't. Usually the children awoke to find candy, nuts, and fruit in their shoes. Later that day relatives might get together, bringing a cake or other gift of food.

On December 24, the *Weihnachtsmann* arrived. *Weihnachts-*

mann means *Christmas Man.* As in West Germany, the Christmas Man could be an intimidating figure at first. But soon he would reach into his sack and bring out a gift for each child. The Christmas Man is similar in appearance to Santa Claus.

Prior to Germany's reunification, Christmas trees were inexpensive and nearly every family could afford one. They usually cost about 15 East German marks —about U.S. $3. Shopping for a Christmas tree was always a family affair in East Germany, and the children especially enjoyed it. Families chose their tree with great care, selecting the green-est, tallest one with the fullest branches.

In the days leading up to Christmas, many East Germans shopped at stores that specialized in Western merchandise. There they could buy hard-to-get items such as electronic equipment, motorized toys, stereos, television sets, and clothing. They could also choose from a great variety of West German candies. The merchandise at these stores was top quality, in contrast to the merchandise found at most East German stores. But the specialty shops refused to accept anything but West German marks, so only

A young German boy discovers all the enchantment of the Christmas season in a special gift from Father Christmas.

people whose West German relatives sent them money could shop at these stores.

At their Christmas fairs, East Germans could buy nearly everything they needed for Christmas festivities, including sweets, ornaments, trees, candles, and wreaths. Before reunification, the state subsidized these fairs, and they were a very inexpensive form of entertainment. But like nearly everything else in Germany today, the prices at the Christmas fairs have risen dramatically. A much wider range of merchandise, however, is now available.

Even under Communist rule, East Berlin was beautifully deco-

rated during Christmas. The city was bright with twinkling lights, its streets lined with colorful streamers. Everyone in East Berlin visited the Christmas fairs, to shop and eat and take pleasure in the season.

On Christmas Eve, East Germans began their final preparations. Cooks started preparing the Christmas feast early in the day. Christmas dinner was much like West German fare, but simpler and less extravagant. Roast goose was served, but stuffing might consist simply of apples. Red cabbage was also a popular dish. The more elaborate West German dishes required ingredients that were beyond the means of most East Germans. But apples, nuts, and cookies were readily available.

On December 24, the family decorated the tree, starting in the mid-afternoon. Like their West German neighbors, they used tinsel, colored lights, candles, figurines, and baked decorations. When the tree was finished and the lights were all turned on, the whole family might join in singing "O Tannenbaum."

East Germans enjoyed yet another treat on Christmas Eve. On this one night the state permitted the broadcast of Western films. Every Christmas Eve, East German television stations showed the most popular European and American films of the year. And East Germans, who faced such difficulties attending church services, may have taken comfort in this special event.

A World-Famous Tradition of Arts and Crafts

For generations, German artists and craft workers have captured the magic and delight of the Christmas season in one-of-a-kind folk art creations. From wooden nutcrackers to blown-glass ornaments, each has brought joy to people throughout the country and all over the world.

Perhaps most renowned of all are the blown-glass ornaments from the tiny village of Lauscha. Situated about 60 miles (97 kilometers) north of Nuremberg in the Thuringian Forest, Lauscha became the birthplace of the shiny glass balls that have delighted children and adults for more than a century. During the 1500's, small groups of Protestant glass blowers settled in this storybook town to escape religious persecution in the historical German region of Swabia. The artisans chose Lauscha because the surrounding region had an abundance of sand, wood, and limestone—all important ingredients for their trade.

In the mid-1800's, the glass blowers in Lauscha began to make the delicate blown-glass ornaments for which they became world famous. Perched on a high stool and hunched over his bench in the tiny Werkstatt (workshop) attached to his cottage, each glass blower created the magnificently detailed, paper-thin glass ornaments that are so prized by collectors today.

Sitting over a flame hot enough to melt glass was hot, demanding work—even in winter's cold. But the glass blowers and their families were accustomed to hard labor. A family working eight to fifteen hours a day, six days a week, could make between 300 and 600 ornaments a year.

A glass blower creates delicate Christmas tree ornaments in the traditional way.

An artisan paints bright red cheeks on a giant nutcracker.

In the early days, a glass blower would feed the hot flame by pumping an inflated goatskin bag under his arm, all the while pushing and pulling free-blown glass bubbles into a variety of shapes. Later, workers used knee-operated bellows placed under their workbenches to keep the fire going. In 1867, when Lauscha built its first gas works, glass blowers at last had a steady, easily adjustable flame with which to work. This made it possible for them to create large, thin-walled bubbles of glass.

For each ornament a glass blower was making, a helper—most often his wife—would "silver" the inside with a special solution. This solution was a combination of silver nitrate, quicklime, and milk sugar, and each glass blower took great pride in creating his own secret formula.

Silvering an ornament involved filling each newly blown ball one-quarter full with the solution and then shaking it. To make sure that the solution coated the ball evenly, the glass blower's wife would have to dip it in hot water several times. Then she would hang up each ornament to dry in the rafters over the stove. After the silvered ornaments

were dry—usually the next day—they were taken down and dipped into colored lacquers. After dipping, they were hung up to dry once again.

Among the most admired ornaments were blown-glass Christmas "treetops," a series of balls one above the other, with a spike on top. Each of these treetops was blown from a single piece of glass.

By the 1890's, glass blowers also began to use **Formsachen** (molds) to create exquisite ornaments in a variety of shapes and colors. Among the most popular forms were pine cones and birds with spun glass tails.

A baker puts the finishing touches on his culinary creations.

Although thousands upon thousands of blown-glass ornaments were created, each one managed to reflect the unique imagination and individual artistry of the glass blower who created it. From tiny trumpets and lyres to elaborate birds and balloons decorated with tinsel, cotton batting, and even crushed glass, these delicate masterpieces are important, endearing examples of German folk art which could never be duplicated by machine. To-day, only a few elderly artisans still create these wondrous, fragile balls in the traditional manner, using many of the old molds.

In the 1700's, even before the glass blowers in Lauscha began making Christmas tree ornaments, German tinsmiths in Nuremberg created tiny tin ornaments in many different geometric shapes, each designed to reflect the glimmering candlelight of the Christmas trees. Nuremberg artisans also crafted intricate ornaments from thin, shiny wire.

No less in demand were the wax-cast ornaments, first exported from Germany to America as early as 1800, but most popular later in that century. One popular type of wax ornament was made in the shape of an angel, with cardboard wings and a gown of ribbon garland. Between 1880 and 1910, artists in the Dresden-Leipzig region created little silver-and-gold embossed cardboard Christmas tree ornaments. And the wood carvers in the mountains of southern Germany created charming small wooden toys.

Today, "icicles" appear on Christmas trees the world over, and they, too, originated in Germany. The original icicles—thin strips of silver foil that could be draped over Christmas tree branches—were first made in Nuremberg in 1878. Today's icicles are made out of silver-colored synthetic materials.

Some of these original creations have endured through the years to bring joy to today's families. But another form of creative expression has never been meant to last long, and that is the culinary delights created by German bakers. These delicious baked goods include **Springerle** (cookies with raised designs) and **Stollen**, which are fruit loaves flavored with raisins, almonds, currants, and candied fruits and shaped in the form of the Christ child in His manger. The Nuremberg region, which was the center of the country's spice trade during the Middle Ages, became famous for its gingerbread.

The most famous German sweet of all—marzipan—was brought back by the Crusaders from the Near East. The lovely confection has since become famous all over the world as a special German treat.

A craft worker assembles a pyramid tree.

"On the second day of Christmas . . ."

The German people enjoy Christmas so much that they have extended it one more day. The "Second Day of Christmas"—December 26—is a legal holiday, celebrated much like Christmas Day itself. And if this second day follows such German traditions as the Christmas tree and the Advent wreath, it may be just a matter of time before the rest of the world joins the continued celebration.

For most families, December 26 is a time to relax with friends and relatives, to spend time with the children, or admire beautiful Nativity scenes in the churches. In the evening, many people go out to dinner or the theater. Others get together with friends at Christmas parties.

A little German girl wears a sweet look of contentment after discovering her presents under the Christmas tree.

December 26 is also St. Stephen's Day. Saint Stephen was the first Christian martyr. Since he is also the patron saint of horsemen, this is a favorite holiday among horse breeders, and many villages and towns in southern Germany organize mounted processions in his honor. Saint Stephen is believed to protect horses against disease, so many people have their horses blessed on this "Second Day of Christmas." The Roman Catholic Church holds special services on St. Stephen's Day.

The entire period between December 25 and January 6 constitutes the Twelve Nights or *Die zwölf Rauhnächte* (Twelfth Tide) in Germany. During this time, many Germans have observed certain ancient customs. In the south, not so long ago, people used to burn incense to ward off against evil spirits. In eastern Bavaria, it was customary for a father and son to carry burning coals in a censer through their house.

Legend has it that if a man lies in a coffin during the Twelve

Villagers wearing grotesque masks prepare to drive away evil spirits during **Rauhnächte** *(Smoke Nights).*

Nights, someone from the village will die each month throughout the year. But it is not an entirely gloomy time. Many happy endings may also be foretold during the Twelve Nights. Young women who want to know the identity of their future husband throw their shoes into a pear tree twelve times. If a young woman's shoes stay up there just once, it means she will marry the man of her dreams.

In some parts of the country, people say that spirits are roaming the land on a *Wilde Jagd* (wild hunt) to haunt the living. Many superstitious practices were thought to protect people from such evil spirits, and some of these old customs still linger. In some areas, the locals hold *Rauhnächte* (Smoke Nights) to drive out the spirits. They build fires and burn incense to create as much smoke as possible. Then, wearing grotesque costumes, they scream, shout, and make the sign of the cross. Few people really believe in such things these days, but the Rauhnächte custom continues because it is such great fun.

The Twelve Days of Christmas are also significant to the German people. According to tradition, each of these days foreshadows one of the months in the year ahead. For example, the first day of Christmas indicates how the month of January will fare, and the second day predicts February's events. If Christmas Day is colder than usual, you could expect that January would be too. If the Second Day of Christmas is cloudy, then February will bring bad news.

People also believe that dreams are especially rich with premonitions during this period. "What a man dreams between Christmas and New Year's is fulfilled," according to an old German proverb. But not all dreams are welcome. Bad dreams or nightmares during this time mean that the year ahead will be a rocky one, and caution is advised.

> *"The entire period between December 25 and January 6 constitutes the Twelve Nights or* **Die zwölf Rauhnächte** *(Twelfth Tide) in Germany."*

In Bavaria, the Twelve Days are known as the "Quiet Twelve Days" because, in the past, all work stopped at this time. Washing, cleaning, baking, and spinning were forbidden. Today, the Twelve Days are still a time when most people relax.

New Year's Eve Predictions

The best night for fortunetelling, however, is New Year's Eve. Many ancient methods of peering into the future have once again become popular in Germany. Perhaps the most widespread is the custom of *Bleigiessen,* when

New Year's Eve partygoers stroke a live pig for good luck. Pigs and chimney sweeps— also a symbol of good luck— were often seen at New Year's Eve celebrations.

people pour molten lead into water. The lead forms odd shapes in the water, and these shapes are supposed to predict the future. For instance, if the lead looks like an airplane, the person is going on a long trip. If it looks like a house, the person may be moving. But most of the fun comes from simply guessing what the lumps look like.

Single women watch the hissing lumps of lead carefully. The lumps are supposed to indicate the name and occupation of their future husband—that is, if anyone knows how to read lead lumps.

Holding the lumps in front of a candle and studying the

shadows they cast on the wall is said to provide a more accurate reading of the future. Many women simply gaze into the firelight and try to envision the man they will marry. In some parts of Germany, young women lie on the floor and toss their shoes backward over their head, carefully noting what direction the toe of the shoe is pointing in. Their future bridegroom will eventually arrive from that direction.

Some people stick a pin randomly on a page of the Bible on New Year's Day. The verse the pin touches is supposed to have special significance for the pin thrower in the coming year.

Few people today seriously believe that molten lead can predict the future or that these other fortunetelling methods really work. But they do provide a great deal of entertainment for many people.

New Year's Eve Celebrations

New Year's Eve—or St. Sylvester's in Germany—is named after Pope Sylvester, the Roman Catholic saint who is honored on December 31.

During the days leading to New Year's, the German people wish each other *einen guten Rutsch* (a good slide into the new year). No sooner has the Second Day of Christmas ended than merchants clear away their Christmas decorations and put their New Year's merchandise on display. The windows are full of colorful streamers, squeakers, firecrackers, and special doughnuts called *Krapfen*.

Throughout Germany, people drive out the old year with as much noise as they can make. This custom extends from the North Sea to the Alps, from the smallest hamlet to the largest city. Everywhere there are gun salutes, fireworks, flares, and rockets shooting up into the night sky. In the Alps, the local riflemen's association fires off

Shopkeepers stock up on fireworks in preparation for New Year's Eve celebrations.

Spectacular fireworks displays light up the skies over cities and towns throughout Germany as merrymakers ring in the new year.

the gun salute. In other areas, single men fulfill this function.

Many years ago, the Prince of Hesse claimed that the custom of shooting off fireworks was "foolish." And so in 1711, he banned the custom. But the people paid no attention, and continued to celebrate New Year's Eve with just as much noise and merrymaking as ever.

Germans usually gather with close friends at parties and dances to ring in the new year and say good-by to the old. During the evening, they'll serve carp or herring salad, followed by a hot wine punch that sometimes includes fruit. *Feuerzangenbowle* (fire tongs punch), a sort of flaming punch, may also be served. To make Feuerzangenbowle, sugar cones are suspend-

ed over the punch bowl, doused with alcohol, and then lit so that the alcohol-drenched sugar drips into the hot wine. But when midnight draws near, Germans put aside the delicious punch and toast the New Year with champagne.

At the stroke of midnight, church bells ring and Germans everywhere raise their glasses to wish each other *"Prost Neujahr!"* ("Happy New Year!") Outside, fireworks have already begun to light up the sky. Shrill rockets whistle, then release their thunderous booms as everyone gathers for the display.

In some towns, trombonists literally "blow in" the New Year with a concert from the church tower. In Bavaria, people turn out all the lights just before midnight, and turn them on again when the clock strikes twelve. In the Alps, they crack whips, fire small cannons, and shoot off guns. And people on the North Frisian Islands go from house to house for cookies and punch. But in every celebration, eyes are bright with high hopes for the year to come.

Epiphany, Twelfth Night, Festival of the Three Kings

Epiphany, which is observed on January 6, is a religious holiday commemorating that day long ago when the Three Wise Men—or the Three Kings—paid tribute to the infant Jesus. According to the Bible, they followed a bright star to the town of Bethlehem, where the infant lay in his mother's arms. It is also the day when St. John the Baptist is said to have baptized Christ as an adult.

Epiphany marks the official end of the Christmas season. The Twelve Days and the Twelve Nights are over, and the daylight is visibly longer. People take down their Christmas trees and decorations. Many of these decorations are heirlooms, which are carefully packed and stored away. School vacation ends for many children on this day, and many offices close. In some federal states, January 6 is an official holiday, and shops and malls are closed.

In Christian countries, Epiphany was once considered a more significant holiday than

Musicians "blow in" the new year for crowds in Munich.

A group of star singers dressed as the Three Wise Men assemble outside a hillside chalet before setting about their rounds through neighboring villages.

Christmas. For centuries, church leaders held to the belief that the day on which the Christ child was recognized as the Son of God deserved more attention.

For the German people, the festival of Epiphany gained even greater significance in 1164, when the remains of the Three Wise Men were brought to the Cologne Cathedral and a shrine was erected in their honor. Cologne then became an important pilgrimage site for Christians from surrounding regions.

Germans today celebrate Epiphany with a mixture of pagan traditions and Christian rituals. In southern Bavaria, people often call the Epiphany "Berchta's Day." Berchta was a goddess in old Germanic folklore. A goddess known as "Mother Holda" is ceremoniously burned on this day at Eichsfeld.

In some areas of Germany, people celebrate a Festival of the Three Kings. Many towns and villages hold balls, and people in the Rhineland crown a "Bean King" and "Bean Queen." The "royals" are usually selected at a big party. Before the party, a cook bakes a bean in each of two doughnuts. According to tradition, if one bean is found during the party by a single man and the other by a single woman, these two—who become the

Bean King and Queen—will eventually marry. This royal couple gives all sorts of ridiculous orders to the rest of the party guests. But later the Bean King and Queen must entertain their guests. This custom dates back to the Middle Ages, in England, when the Bean King had to fulfill certain religious functions.

Pagan superstitions have also become part of Three Kings' Day ritual. If you don't eat well on this day, for example, evil spirits will slip knives through your stomach. Divining rods cut on Three Kings' Day are said to be more effective in helping their users locate gold, silver, and water.

In southern and western Germany, people consecrate salt and pieces of chalk. They give

A Bavarian boy holds his star aloft as he and three companions process through a snow-dusted field.

the salt to animals to lick, and write the traditional names of the Three Kings—Gaspar, Melchior, and Balthasar—outside their homes. The animals and home are said to be protected through this ritual.

If you are traveling through the town of Pottenstein, Bavaria, on January 6, you might see a Procession of Light. In this procession, people carry torches and lanterns through the streets, while huge bonfires burn on the mountaintops in the distance. Floodlights illuminate the local castle, bells ring, and star shells explode overhead. After the fanfare and revelry, people attend church services. In other Bavarian towns, young boys and girls called "Star Singers" go singing through the streets in groups or

a procession. One singer carries a lighted star on a pole while the rest—costumed as the Three Kings—carry incense, myrrh, and long staffs. On their way, they sing "Star Songs"—a tuneful good-by to the season. Often they carry a crèche that is later given to some needy family.

The blessing of homes is another widespread custom during Epiphany. On this day, church pastors accompanied by two ministrants visit the homes of their congregations. One of the ministrants carries holy water, and the other carries a vessel of incense. When swung about, the vessel emits the sweet fragrance of burning incense.

Upon arrival at the home of a parishioner, the pastor first blesses the family by making the

Although the festive Christmas season may be over, these German children still manage to have fun on a snowy day.

sign of the cross. Then, he prays for the peace and security of each family member. Finally, he writes "G+M+B" on either the door posts or ceiling beams. The initials stand for the names of the Three Wise Men—Gaspar, Melchior, and Balthasar.

Each of the wise men has his own special duty to perform to ensure the security of the household. Gaspar, who brought gold to the Christ Child, makes sure that the family never lacks their daily bread. Melchior, whose gift was incense, watches over the house lest the fire—and human life—be extinguished. And Balthasar, who carried myrrh to Bethlehem, assures God's protection.

After Epiphany, several weeks of cold winter lie ahead. Life returns to normal, and people begin to look forward to spring. The biggest celebration in Germany has at last come to an end. But for a magical month, everyone has had a very Fröhliche Weihnachten.

German Crafts

Gingerbread House

(Note: It may take several days to complete this project, so it's a good idea to start it on a weekend.)

Materials

- *one batch Gingerbread Dough (see recipe below)*
- *one 10" x 15" sheet heavy paper*
- *fine-line black pen*
- *ruler*
- *scissors*

- *rolling pin*
- *small sharp knife*
- *one batch snow-white icing*
- *pastry bag with #3 decorator's tip*
- *one 12" x 12" sheet cardboard*

- *aluminum foil*
- *several cups of assorted candy, including hard candy, peppermint rounds, candy canes, gumdrops, and so on, for decorating the house*

Recipes

Gingerbread Dough
- *1 cup firmly packed brown sugar*
- *$\frac{1}{3}$ cup shortening*
- *1 $\frac{1}{2}$ cups dark molasses*
- *$\frac{3}{4}$ cup cold water*
- *7 cups all-purpose flour*
- *2 tsp. baking soda*
- *1 tsp. salt*
- *2 tsp. ground ginger*
- *1 tsp. ground cloves*
- *1 tsp. ground cinnamon*

In a large bowl, mix together brown sugar, shortening, and molasses until well blended. Stir in remaining ingredients. Cover and refrigerate for at least 4 hours.

Snow-white Icing
- *3 egg whites*
- *$\frac{1}{2}$ tsp. cream of tartar*
- *1 pound confectioners' sugar*

Combine egg whites and cream of tartar in a mixing bowl. Beat with an electric mixer on low speed until frothy. Gradually add confectioner's sugar, mixing well after each addition. After all sugar has been added, beat icing on high speed for 7 to 10 minutes. Icing is ready when a knife drawn through it leaves a clear path that holds its shape.

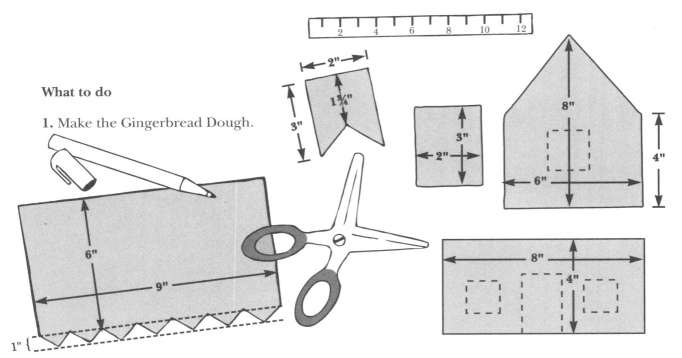

What to do

1. Make the Gingerbread Dough.

2. While the dough is in the refrigerator, outline the pattern pieces of the house on the heavy paper, using the dimensions shown above. Cut out the patterns. Note: On long side pattern, you will only cut out the windows and door from the dough once. The back of the house will have no windows or door.

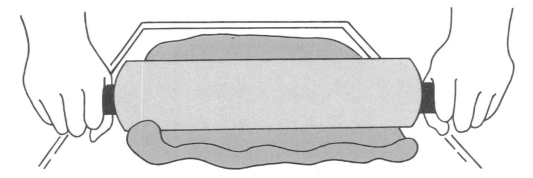

3. When the dough is ready, divide it in half. Leave one half in the refrigerator. On a lightly greased cookie sheet, roll out the other half with a rolling pin to $\frac{1}{16}$" thickness.

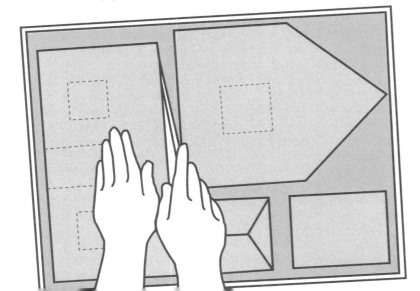

4. Lay out as many lightly floured pattern pieces as will fit on the cookie sheet of dough.

5. Cut around the outline of each pattern piece with the small sharp knife. Remove the scrap dough and save it for making shutters, doors, steps, and other decorations you might want to use on the outside of the house.

6. Again using the knife, cut out windows and doors on the front, back, and side patterns of dough.

7. Bake the gingerbread at 375 °F until no indentation remains when dough is pressed with a finger—about 10 minutes for large pieces, 5 to 6 minutes for smaller ones.

8. While first pieces are baking and cooling, prepare a second cookie sheet and roll out, cut, and bake until you have made two each of all pattern pieces, which will be 10 pieces altogether, and any shutters, doors, or steps you want to use. Cool pieces completely before decorating.

9. Prepare the Snow-white Icing. Spoon the icing into a pastry bag fitted with a #3 decorator's tip. The icing is used as "glue" to hold the house together.

10. First join one side wall to one end piece by piping icing along one edge of the end piece and pressing the side piece into the icing. Press in place until it holds. Allow the frosting to dry before handling the joined pieces; this can take from 30 minutes to 4 hours.

11. While waiting for frosting to dry, prepare a base on which to put the house. Cover the 12" x 12" sheet of cardboard with aluminum foil.

12. Continue joining pieces until the house is complete. Reinforce the seams with more icing, and pipe icing along the base of the house to help connect it to the aluminum foil base. Allow house to dry completely.

13. To make the chimney, join together the four chimney pieces, as you did to make the house. Once dry, attach the chimney to the roof using icing. Allow the entire house to dry before decorating it.

14. Decorate the house as you wish. Use icing to affix candy decorations and to connect shutters, doors, steps, and other gingerbread pieces.

(Note: Tempting as it may be, do not eat any gingerbread house that is more than a few days old. You may wish to make two gingerbread houses—one for eating right away and one for decorating!)

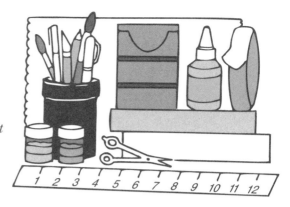

Personalized Advent Calendar

(Note: You may want to complete this project in November so that your calendar is ready when it's time to open the first window.)

Materials

- *two 8 ½" x 10" sheets heavy white paper*
- *crayons, markers, or paints*
- *one 12" x 12" sheet cardboard*
- *masking tape*

- *fine-line black pen*
- *ruler*
- *craft knife*
- *manicure scissors*
- *pencil*

- *Christmas catalogs, Christmas stickers or stamps, used Christmas cards, photocopies of photographs of family members' and friends' faces, or anything else that can be used for the pictures to go inside each calendar window*

What to do

1. To make the front surface of the calendar, create a Christmas scene on one side of one of the sheets of heavy white paper, using crayons, markers, or paints. Use your imagination. Some ideas include people holiday shopping, a decorated Christmas tree, and a Nativity scene. Your drawing should cover the entire sheet of paper. If you'd feel more comfortable, draw an outline of your picture first and then color it in.

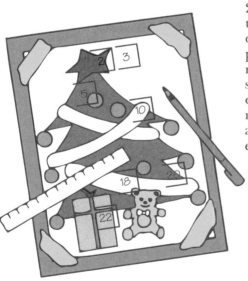

2. Lay your drawing on the center of the cardboard. Tape down the corners to keep it in place. With the pen, print the numbers 1 through 24, very small and scattered over the entire drawing. Make sure the numbers are at least 1¼" apart and at least 1" away from the edges of the drawing.

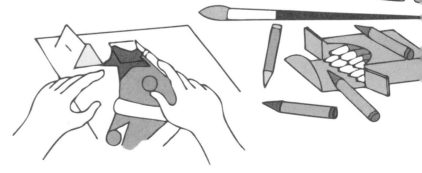

3. With the pen and ruler, begin drawing 1" x 1" window boxes around each number so that the number is in the center of the window. *You need only draw the top, bottom and right side of the window.*

4. Have an adult help you use the craft knife to cut along the window outlines. (Remember to cut only three edges of each window—the left side should stay uncut.) Use the manicure scissors to make the cuts complete, if necessary.

5. Carefully untape the front of the calendar from the cardboard and set it aside. Tape the other sheet of heavy paper to the cardboard, then place the front of the calendar on top of it so that they're exactly even with each other. Tape the front of the calendar in place. Carefully lift each window, and use the pencil to make a small "x" on the bottom sheet of paper. Each "x" should be placed in the center of a window. Remove the front of the calendar and set it aside.

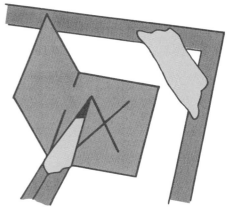

6. Decide what you'd like to use for the 24 pictures that will go on the inside of each window. Some ideas include Christmas stickers or stamps; small pictures of toys and Christmas decorations cut from catalogs; and cutouts from used Christmas cards. (Ask permission before you cut up catalogs or Christmas cards.) Choose only pictures that are no bigger than 1" x 1" square.

7. Glue a picture over each "x" until you've covered all 24 of them.

8. Remove the sheet of pictures from the cardboard and then place the front of the calendar over it; be sure the sheet of pictures is right-side up. Tape the two sheets together along the edges.

9. For each day from December 1 through December 24, open up the window on the calendar that corresponds with the day of the month. Crease each window along the top so it stays open.

10. After Christmas, carefully close all the windows on your calendar. Store the calendar flat so that you can use it again next Christmas.

German recipes

Cinnamon Stars

2 cups powdered sugar
5 egg whites
dash of salt
2 tsp. ground cinnamon
1 tsp. grated lemon zest
1 lb. ground unblanched almonds
powdered sugar

Preheat oven to 300 °F. Sift sugar; set aside. In a large bowl, beat egg whites and salt until stiff but not dry. Continue beating while adding sifted sugar, cinnamon, and lemon zest. Set aside ⅓ of the mixture. Fold almonds into the remaining batter.

Dust a pastry board with powdered sugar. With your fingers, press dough to ⅓-inch thickness. Do not use a rolling pin. If dough is sticky, dust your palms with powdered sugar. Cut dough with a star-shaped cookie cutter. Glaze with reserved egg mixture. Bake on a greased cookie sheet for 20 minutes.

Makes about 4 dozen cookies.

Schokoladenmakronen (Chocolate Macaroons)

4 egg whites
½ cup sugar
2 cups finely chopped almonds
5 squares unsweetened chocolate, finely grated
3 tbsp. water
¼ tsp. ground cinnamon
dash *each* ground allspice, cardamom,
    and nutmeg

Preheat oven to 300 °F. In a large bowl, beat egg whites until stiff. While still beating, gradually add sugar. Fold in almonds, chocolate, water, and spices. Drop mixture by teaspoonfuls onto waxed-paper-lined cookie sheets. Bake for 20 to 25 minutes. Cool on racks. Store cookies in a tightly sealed container.

Makes about 3 dozen cookies.

Braune Kuchen (Honey Cookies)

1½ cups honey
1 stick margarine
1 cup firmly packed brown sugar
5¾ cups flour
1½ tbsp. powdered sugar
1 egg
¾ cup chopped almonds
3 tbsp. cocoa
1 tsp. *each* ground cloves and cinnamon
¼ tsp. *each* ground nutmeg, cardamom,
    and allspice
1 slightly beaten egg white
chopped almonds, chopped candied cherries,
    and candy sprinkles
flour

Preheat oven to 325 °F. In a 1-quart saucepan, heat honey, margarine, and brown sugar over medium heat, stirring constantly, until well blended. Remove from heat; allow to cool. Meanwhile, in a large bowl, combine flour, powdered sugar, egg, almonds, cocoa, and spices. Stir in cooled honey mixture; mix until smooth and well blended.

Divide dough into three equal parts. On a lightly floured pastry board, roll each section into a thin sheet. Use cookie cutters to cut dough. Bake on greased cookie sheets for about 10 minutes. While cookies are still warm, brush with beaten egg white. Decorate with almonds, candied cherries, or candy sprinkles.

Makes about 6½ dozen cookies.

Pfeffernüsse

2 cups plus 2 tbsp. sifted flour
¾ tsp. baking powder
⅛ tsp. baking soda
dash of salt
¼ tsp. freshly ground pepper
1 tsp. ground cinnamon
¼ tsp. *each* ground nutmeg and
    ground cloves
¼ tsp. anise seeds
1 stick butter
⅓ cup sugar
1 egg
¼ cup finely chopped almonds
1 tbsp. corn syrup
⅓ cup molasses
⅓ cup brandy
juice of 1 lemon
1 tsp. lemon zest
powdered sugar

In a small bowl, sift together flour, baking powder, baking soda, salt, and pepper. Add remaining spices. Set aside.

Using an electric mixer, cream butter and sugar in a large bowl. Add egg and beat until light. Mix in almonds. In a small bowl, combine the corn syrup, molasses, brandy, lemon juice, and lemon zest. Add flour mixture alternately with the corn syrup mixture. Beat well after each addition. Allow dough to sit overnight in bowl lightly covered with a clean kitchen towel.

Preheat oven to 350°F. Roll dough into 1-inch balls. Bake on a greased cookie sheet for 10 to 15 minutes. While the cookies are still warm, roll them in powdered sugar.

Makes about 15 dozen cookies.

Springerle

2 cups powdered sugar
4 eggs
4 cups sifted flour, divided
½ tsp. baking powder
2 tbsp. crushed anise seeds

Sift sugar; set aside. In a medium-sized bowl, beat eggs until light. Gradually add sugar, continuing to beat until creamy. In a separate bowl, sift together 3 cups of the flour and the baking powder. Add flour mixture to egg mixture.

Sprinkle ½ cup of the remaining flour on a pastry board. Turn the dough onto the pastry board and knead in enough flour—about ½ cup more—to stiffen dough. Roll into a rectangle, ⅓-inch thick. Cut into ¾- x 2½-inch bars. If dough is too soft, gradually add more flour. Allow bars to dry uncovered in a cool, dry place for 12 hours.

Preheat oven to 300°F. Sprinkle a greased cookie sheet with crushed anise seeds. Bake bars on cookie sheet for 15 minutes or until the lower halves of the bars are light yellow.

Makes about 5 dozen bars.

Marzipan

1½ cups finely ground almonds
1½ cups powdered sugar
⅛ tsp. almond extract
1 cup grated semisweet chocolate

In a 1-quart saucepan over medium heat, mix almonds, sugar, and almond extract. Heat slightly. Allow mixture to cool. Knead into a dough, adding a little more powdered sugar if necessary. Place dough in an airtight container and let stand overnight. Shape into small balls; roll in grated chocolate.

Makes about ½ pound of candy.

Lebkuchen (Ginger Cookies)

Batter
1 egg
¾ cup firmly packed brown sugar
½ cup dark molasses
½ cup honey
3 tbsp. brandy
1 tsp. fresh lemon juice
½ tsp. grated lemon zest
4 cups flour
½ tsp. *each* baking soda, ground
    ginger, and ground cloves
1 tsp. ground cinnamon
¼ tsp. ground cardamom
½ cup chopped almonds
¼ cup *each* chopped citron and chopped
    candied orange or lemon peel

Lemon Glaze
1 egg white
1 tbsp. fresh lemon juice
dash of salt
1½ cups sifted powdered sugar

In a medium-sized bowl, beat egg until light. Add brown sugar and beat until light and fluffy. Stir in molasses, honey, brandy, lemon juice, and lemon zest. Beat mixture thoroughly; set aside.

In a separate bowl, stir together flour, baking soda, and spices. Blend into honey mixture. Stir in almonds, citron, and candied peel. Refrigerate dough overnight.

Preheat oven to 350°F. Divide dough in half. On a lightly floured pastry board, roll each half to ⅓-inch thickness. Cut into 3- x 2-inch cookies. Bake on a greased cookie sheet for 10 to 12 minutes. Allow to cool slightly in pan, then remove to rack.

While cookies are baking, prepare Lemon Glaze. In a small bowl, combine egg white, lemon juice, and salt. Stir in powdered sugar. Mix well. Brush cookies with Lemon Glaze while they're still warm.

Makes about 3½ dozen cookies.

Pfefferkuchenpuppen (Spice Cookies)

Batter
⅔ cup honey
½ firmly packed brown sugar
1 stick butter
4¼ cups flour
1¼ tsp. baking powder
3 tbsp. cocoa
½ tsp. *each* ground cinnamon, cardamom,
    allspice, nutmeg, coriander, and black pepper
1 egg
vanilla or chocolate frosting
decorative icings, colored sprinkles
    (purchased at store)

Vanilla or Chocolate Frosting
¾ stick butter or margarine
3 cups powdered sugar
1½ tbsp. milk
1 tbsp. vanilla
6 tbsp. cocoa (if making chocolate frosting)

Preheat oven to 400°F. In a 1-quart saucepan, combine honey, brown sugar, and butter. Heat over medium heat, stirring constantly, until blended; allow to cool slightly. Meanwhile, in a large bowl, combine flour, baking powder, cocoa, and spices. Gradually blend in egg and honey mixture. Knead dough until smooth. Divide dough into three equal parts. On a lightly floured pastry board, roll out each section of dough to ⅛- to ¼-inch thickness. Cut dough with cookie cutters. Bake on a greased cookie sheet for 8 to 10 minutes.

While cookies are baking, prepare frosting. In a small bowl, beat butter or margarine. Gradually add powdered sugar, milk, vanilla, and cocoa (if making chocolate frosting). Beat until light and fluffy.

Frost cookies and use decorative icing and sprinkles to add detail.

Makes 8 dozen cookies.

Spekulatius (Speculaas)

4¼ cups flour
1 cup firmly packed brown sugar
1 stick butter, softened
¾ cup finely grated almonds
2 eggs
1½ tbsp. milk
¼ tsp. salt
½ tsp. ground cloves
1 tsp. ground cinnamon
¼ tsp. *each* ground allspice
    and ground nutmeg
½ cup slivered almonds

In a large bowl, beat together all ingredients except slivered almonds. Cover mixture and refrigerate for 1 hour.

Preheat oven to 325°F. Press dough firmly onto a floured Speculaas mold.* Carefully transfer onto a greased cookie sheet. Repeat with remaining dough. Sprinkle with slivered almonds. Bake for 15 to 20 minutes or until lightly browned.

Makes about 5 dozen cookies.

* Speculaas molds are available in many sizes and shapes. They can be found in gourmet shops and cookware departments.

"S" Butter Cookies

2 cups flour
1 stick room-temperature butter
3 egg yolks
⅓ cup sugar
1 tbsp. lemon zest
1 beaten egg white
sugar

In a medium-sized bowl, mix together flour and next 4 ingredients. Let the mixture stand in a cool, dry place for 30 minutes. Roll out on a floured pastry board to ½-inch thickness. Cut into even strips, then bend strips into the shape of the letter S. Place cookies on a greased cookie sheet and let set in a cool, dry place for another 30 minutes. Brush cookies with beaten egg white. Sprinkle lightly with sugar. Bake in a 400°F oven for about 10 to 12 minutes or until golden brown.

Makes about 2 dozen cookies.

Schokolademuscheln (Chocolate Shells)

3 squares unsweetened chocolate
2 egg whites
¼ cup sugar
¾ cup finely grated almonds
¼ tsp. *each* ground cinnamon and
    ground cloves
sugar

Melt chocolate in a double boiler; do not allow to burn. Remove from heat and let cool. Meanwhile, in a medium-sized bowl, beat egg whites until stiff. Stir in sugar. Add melted chocolate to egg mixture. Stir in almonds, cinnamon, and cloves. Roll dough into small balls, cover with sugar, then press center with thumb. Place on waxed paper; dry overnight. Bake in a 300°F oven for 25 minutes or until golden brown.

Makes about 2 dozen cookies.

Stollen

(Stollen is best when stored in an airtight container for several days before serving.)

3¾ cups flour
½ cup lukewarm milk, divided
1 cup powdered sugar, divided
1 pkg. yeast
1 stick plus 1 tbsp. softened butter
1 egg
½ tsp. salt
1 tsp. vanilla
1 tbsp. rum
pinch of ground cinnamon
1 tbsp. grated lemon zest
1 cup slivered almonds
¼ cup *each* candied orange and
    lemon peel
1¼ cups raisins
½ cup lukewarm milk
1 stick butter, melted
¾ cup powdered sugar
flour

Sift flour into a large mixing bowl. Make a well in the center of the flour and pour in ¼ cup of the milk and ¼ cup of the powdered sugar. Sprinkle in yeast and then dust with a little flour. Allow the yeast to develop for 15 to 20 minutes. Add butter, egg, salt, remaining sugar, vanilla, rum, cinnamon, grated lemon zest, slivered almonds, candied peel, and raisins. Add only enough of the remaining milk to make dough pliable. Knead thoroughly. Cover with a clean, damp dishtowel and let rise overnight.

Preheat oven to 350°F. Knead dough again for 1 minute. Shape into one loaf and place on a large buttered cookie sheet. Push back in any raisins that popped up so they won't scorch during baking. Baste loaf with several tablespoons of milk. Bake for about 50 minutes or until golden brown. Test with a toothpick, which should come out clean when inserted.

Baste the stollen with plenty of butter while it's still hot, then sprinkle with powdered sugar. Repeat until loaf has an even, white surface. This will keep stollen fresh and moist for several weeks.

Makes 1 loaf of about 30 slices.

Schwarzwälder Apfelkuchen (Custard-Apple Torte)

1¼ cups unsifted flour
⅓ cup sugar
1 stick butter or margarine
1 egg yolk
¼ tsp. vanilla
4-5 medium-sized tart cooking apples
    (Macintosh or Granny Smith), peeled,
    cored, and quartered
4 oz. cream cheese, room temperature
¾ cup sugar
1 tsp. vanilla
2 eggs
½ cup half-and-half
¼ tsp. ground nutmeg

Preheat oven to 400°F. To make the pastry, mix flour with sugar in a medium-sized bowl. Cut in butter or margarine until crumbly. In a separate bowl, beat egg yolk with vanilla flavoring. With a fork, stir egg mixture into flour mixture until well combined, then press dough together with your fingers.

Press pastry into the bottom and halfway up the sides of a 9-inch spring-form pan. Using the tines of a fork, score the outside of each apple quarter from end to end, so it looks like a row of thin apple slices. Arrange apples, scored-sides up, in the pastry-lined pan.

In a small mixing bowl, beat cream cheese until fluffy; gradually beat in sugar and vanilla. Add eggs, one at a time, beating well after each one. Beat in half-and-half. Pour egg mixture over apples. Sprinkle with nutmeg. Bake for 50 to 60 minutes, until apples are tender and pastry is well browned. Serve warm or cool.

Makes 6 to 8 servings.

Linzertorte

2 sticks softened butter
1 cup sugar
1 tsp. vanilla
3 egg yolks
2 cups finely ground
   unblanched almonds
1 tbsp. grated lemon zest
1 tsp. ground cinnamon
½ tsp. *each* ground cloves
   and ground nutmeg
2 cups sifted flour
1 20-oz. jar red raspberry preserves
   (Press through a sieve to remove
   the seeds, if desired.)
1 slightly beaten egg white
powdered sugar

In a large mixing bowl, cream butter, sugar, and vanilla. Beat in egg yolks, one at a time, beating well after each one. Mix in almonds, lemon zest, and spices. Gradually mix in flour, beating slowly until well combined. Wrap ⅓ of the dough in waxed paper and refrigerate for 30 to 40 minutes.

Preheat oven to 350 °F. Press remaining dough evenly over bottom and sides of a 12½-inch spring-form pan. Spread with ¾ of the preserves. On a floured pastry board, divide remaining dough into 16 even pieces. Roll each under your fingers to form a long strand. Place strands over preserves to form a latticework. Brush with beaten egg white.

Bake torte for 35 to 40 minutes, until crust is golden brown. Let cool in pan about 10 minutes, then pop out the bottom of the pan and place the torte on a serving plate. Spoon some of the remaining preserves into each square formed by the latticework. Cool; sift powdered sugar over the top just before serving.

Makes 10 to 12 servings.

Schnitz–oder Hutzelbrot (Fruit Bread)

1 cup chopped dried pears
1 cup chopped dried prunes
4 cups water
2 tbsp. shortening
1 tbsp. sugar
1 tsp. salt
2 pkgs. dry yeast
5½ cups flour
½ tsp. ground cinnamon
¼ tsp. ground cloves
½ cup raisins
½ cup chopped walnuts

In a 2-quart saucepan, cook dried fruit in water according to package directions. Drain well, reserving 2 cups liquid. Set fruit aside. Stir shortening, sugar, and salt into reserved liquid. Cool to lukewarm. In a large mixing bowl, combine yeast, 2 cups flour, cinnamon, and cloves. Add reserved liquid mixture and beat at low speed for 30 seconds, scraping sides of bowl constantly. Beat 3 minutes more at high speed. With a wooden spoon, stir in drained fruit, raisins, walnuts, and enough of the remaining flour to make a moderately stiff dough. Transfer to a lightly floured pastry board. Knead until smooth and elastic, about 8 minutes. Place in a greased bowl, turning once to grease surface. Let dough rise in a warm, dry place until it doubles in size, about 1 hour.

Preheat oven to 375 °F. Punch down dough; divide in half. Cover and let rest for 10 minutes. Shape into two loaves. Place into greased loaf pans. Let rise in a warm place until almost double in size, about 30 minutes. Bake 35 to 40 minutes or until golden brown. (Cover loosely with foil during the last 15 minutes of baking time to prevent overbrowning.)

Makes two loaves of about 20 slices each.

German Carols

How Brightly Shines the Morning Star

Philip Nicolai, 1598
Translation: William Mercer

Philip Nicolai, 1598
Arranged by: J.S. Bach, ca 1730

How bright-ly shines the morn-ing star, With mer-cy beam-ing
O Right-eous Branch, O Jes-se's Rod! Thou Son of Man and

from a-far; The host of heav'n re-joi-ces;
Son of God! We, too, will lift our voi-ces:

Je-sus, Je-sus! Ho-ly, ho-ly, yet most low-ly,

Draw Thou near us; Great Em-man-uel, come and hear us.

From *The International Book of Christmas Carols* arranged and translated by Walter Ehret and George K. Evans.
Copyright © 1963, 1980 by Walter Ehret and George K. Evans. Reprinted with permission.

Lo, How a Rose E'er Blooming

Traditional German
Translation: Theodore Baker, 1894

Kölner Gesangbuch, 1599
Harmonization: Michael Praetorius, 1609 [WE]

Andante

1. Lo, how a Rose e'er bloom-ing From ten-der stem hath sprung! Of Jes-se's lin-eage com-ing, As men of old have sung. It came, a flow-'ret bright, A-mid the cold of win-ter, When half-spent was the night.

2. Isaiah 'twas foretold it,
The Rose I have in mind,
With Mary we behold it,
The Virgin Mother kind.
To show God's love aright,
She bore to men a Savior
When half-spent was the night.

3. This Flow'r, whose fragrance tender
With sweetness fills the air,
Dispels with glorious splendor
The darkness ev'rywhere.
True man, yet very God;
From sin and death He saves us,
And lightens ev'ry load.

From *The International Book of Christmas Carols* arranged and translated by Walter Ehret and George K. Evans.
Copyright © 1963, 1980 by Walter Ehret and George K. Evans. Reprinted with permission.

Break Forth, O Beauteous Heavenly Light

Johann Rist, 1607–1667
Translation: J. Troutbeck, 1832–1899

Johann Schop, died ca 1664
Adapted and
Harmonized by J.S. Bach

Break forth, O beau-teous heav'n-ly light, And ush-er in the morn-ing; Ye shep-herds, shrink not with af-fright, But hear the an-gel's warn-ing. This Child, now weak in in-fan-cy, Our con-fi-dence and joy shall be, The pow'r of Sa-tan break-ing, Our peace e-ter-nal mak-ing.

From *The International Book of Christmas Carols* arranged and translated by Walter Ehret and George K. Evans.
Copyright © 1963, 1980 by Walter Ehret and George K. Evans. Reprinted with permission.

From Heaven Above to Earth I Come

Martin Luther, 1535
Translation: Catherine Winkworth, 1829–1878

Melody Published by Leipzig, 1539
(Attributed to Martin Luther)
Harmonization J.S. Bach, 1685–1750

Andante

1. From heav'n a-bove to earth I come, To bear good news to ev-'ry home, Glad ti-dings of great joy I bring, Where of I now will glad-ly sing.

2. To you this night is born a Child
Of Mary, chosen mother mild;
This little Child, of lowly birth,
Shall be the joy of all the earth.

3. Glory to God in the highest heav'n,
Who unto us his Son hath giv'n!
While angels sing with pious mirth,
A glad New Year to all the earth.

From *The International Book of Christmas Carols* arranged and translated by Walter Ehret and George K. Evans.
Copyright © 1963, 1980 by Walter Ehret and George K. Evans. Reprinted with permission.

Acknowledgments

Cover: © M.u.H., Bavaria Bildagentur

1: © Hackenberg, ZEFA
2: © ZEFA
3: © Hackenberg, ZEFA
7: © R. Waldkirch, Interfoto
8: © Wiersma, Bavaria Bildagentur
10: Eastfoto from Sovfoto
11-13: Interfoto
14: © Schulze-Berka, Interfoto
17: © ZEFA
18: *Adoration of the Magi* (about 1225) illuminated manuscript page from a German Gospel Lectionary by an unknown artist (Granger Collection)
19: © DPA from Photoreporters, Inc.
20: © A. Gruber, Bavaria Bildagentur
21: Sammlung Friedrich Rauch from Interfoto
22: Interfoto
23: © DPA from Photoreporters, Inc.
24: Eastfoto from Sovfoto
27: © DPA from Photoreporters, Inc.
28: © Starfoto from ZEFA
29-30: © DPA from Photoreporters, Inc.
31: © ZEFA
32: © Braennhage, ZEFA
33: © German Information Center
34: © Archinger, Interfoto
35: © DPA from Photoreporters, Inc.
36: © Ingo Wandmacher, Interfoto

37: © W. Brandlein, Okapia
38: German Information Center: © Laemmerer, Bavaria Bildagentur
39: German Information Center
41-42: Interfoto
43: © Benelux, ZEFA
44: © Bahmuller, Bavaria Bildagentur; © Lorenz, Bavaria Bildagentur
46: © DPA from Photoreporters, Inc.
47-48: Eastfoto from Sovfoto
50-51: © DPA from Photoreporters, Inc.
52: Interfoto
53: Eastfoto from Sovfoto
55: © ZEFA
56: © Interfoto
58: © DPA from Photoreporters, Inc.
60: © Paul Gluske, Bavaria Bildagentur
61: © DPA from Photoreporters, Inc.
62: © Matte, ZEFA
63: © Matheisl, Bavaria Bildagentur
64: © Interfoto
65-69: Carol Brozman

Woodcut illustrations: Carol Brozman
Advent calendar: K+H Benser, ZEFA; illustrations by Carol Brozman
Recipe cards: WORLD BOOK photos by Dale DeBolt

MANHATTAN PUBLIC LIBRARY DIST